D0267329

MARRAKESH
ENCOUNTER

ALISON BING

Marrakesh Encounter

Published by Lonely Planet Publications Pty Ltd
ABN 36 005 607 983

Australia	Locked Bag 1, Footscray,
(Head Office)	Vic 3011
	☎ 03 8379 8000 fax 03 8379 8111
USA	150 Linden St, Oakland, CA 94607
	☎ 510 250 6400
	toll free 800 275 8555
	fax 510 893 8572
UK	2nd fl, 186 City Rd
	London EC1V 2NT
	☎ 020 7106 2100 fax 020 7106 2101
Contact	talk2us@lonelyplanet.com
	lonelyplanet.com/contact

This title was commissioned in Lonely Planet's Melbourne office and produced by: **Commissioning Editor** David Carroll **Coordinating Editor** Victoria Harrison **Coordinating Cartographer** Xavier Di Toro **Coordinating Layout Designer** Yvonne Bischofberger **Senior Editor** Susan Paterson **Managing Editor** Brigitte Ellemor **Managing Cartographers** Shahara Ahmed, Adrian Persoglia **Managing Layout Designer** Jane Hart **Assisting Editor** Pat Kinsella **Cover Research** Naomi Parker **Internal Image Research** Rebecca Skinner **Thanks to** Jessica Boland, Helen Christinis, Ryan Evans, Lisa Knights

10 9 8 7 6 5 4 3 2 1

2nd edition
ISBN 9781741793161
Printed in China

Acknowledgement Marrakesh maps based on the map Marrakech! My Map © 2010 Editions Bab Sabaa

FSC
www.fsc.org

MIX
Paper from
responsible sources
FSC™ C021741

Lonely Planet and the Lonely Planet logo are trademarks of Lonely Planet and are registered in the US Patent and Trademark Office and in other countries.

Lonely Planet does not allow its name or logo to be appropriated by commercial establishments, such as retailers, restaurants or hotels. Please let us know of any misuses: www.lonelyplanet.com/ip.

© Lonely Planet 2011. All rights reserved.

HOW TO USE THIS BOOK
Colour-Coding & Maps
Colour-coding is used for symbols on maps and in the text that they relate to (eg all eating venues on the maps and in the text are given a green knife and fork symbol). Each neighbourhood also gets its own colour, and this is used down the edge of the page and throughout that neighbourhood section.

Although the authors and Lonely Planet have taken all reasonable care in preparing this book, we make no warranty about the accuracy or completeness of its content and, to the maximum extent permitted, disclaim all liability arising from its use.

Send us your feedback We love to hear from travellers – your comments keep us on our toes and help make our books better. Our well-travelled team reads every word on what you loved or loathed about this book. Although we cannot reply individually to postal submissions, we always guarantee that your feedback goes straight to the appropriate authors, in time for the next edition. Each person who sends us information is thanked in the next edition, and the most useful submissions are rewarded with a free book.

Visit **lonelyplanet.com** to submit your updates and suggestions or to ask for help. Our award-winning website also features inspirational travel stories, news and discussions.

Note: We may edit, reproduce and incorporate your comments in Lonely Planet products such as guidebooks, websites and digital products, so let us know if you don't want your comments reproduced or your name acknowledged. For a copy of our privacy policy visit lonelyplanet.com/privacy.

ALISON BING

When she's not methodically sampling every *mechoui* lamb roast in Marrakesh, diligently inspecting riad rooftop sunsets or personally testing hammam steam levels, Alison co-authors Lonely Planet's *Morocco, California, USA* and *Italy* guides. Alison has a background in Islamic art, architecture and North African political economy from the American University in Cairo, and holds a masters degree from the Fletcher School of Law and Diplomacy, a program of Tufts and Harvard Universities – respectable diplomatic credentials she regularly undermines with opinionated art, food and culture commentary for newspapers, magazines and radio.

ALISON'S THANKS

Shukran bezzef (many thanks) to editorial *maâlem* (expert) David Carroll for making this guide possible; the editorial team for making it snappy; publishing director Geoff Stringer, for personally road-testing last edition; and cartographer Adrian Persoglia, who makes 3000 *derbs* (winding alleys) seem doable.

Allah yhrem waldikum (blessings upon your parents) to Marrakesh experts Souad Boudeiry, Saïda Chab, Meryanne Loum-Martin, Si Ahmad Nmeis, Mohamed, Omar and Kay Nour and Marrakesh mavens Sahai Burrowes and Sandeep Brar. *Tbarkallalek* (congratulations on your accomplishment) to Marco Flavio Marinucci for magnificent photos capturing the warmth, wit and creativity of Marrakesh. To the people of Marrakesh, who extend a welcome like none other: *allah ykhlef,* may your kindnesses be returned to you tenfold.

Our readers Many thanks to the travellers who wrote to us with helpful hints, useful advice and interesting anecdotes: Annelys, Nadia Asri, Bronny Bennett, Rupert Blum, Maria Goddard, Tom Halat, Emiliana Iovannone, Sherylene Kohiti, Stefan Landolt, Phil Mordecai, Robert Reid, Marian Starkey, Jason Stearns.

Cover photograph A local stands in the front entrance of a house in Marrakesh / Bruce Bi / photolibrary.com. **Internal photographs** All photographs by Lonely Planet Images, and by Marco Flavio Marinucci except p25 Tim Barker; p19 Olivier Cirendini; p70, p110 Brian Cruickshank; p14, p109 Huw Jones; p28 bottom Holger Leue; p130 Jean-Pierre Lescourret; p4, p6 top left, p6 bottom, p8, p15, p18, p23, p28, 98, 104, 125, 136, 139 Doug McKinlay; p73 Mohamed Nour and p10 Geoff Stringer

All images are copyright of the photographers unless otherwise indicated. Many of the images in this guide are available for licensing from **Lonely Planet Images:** www.lonelyplanetimages.com.

It's never a chore, shopping at this small establishment that's like many found in the backstreets

CONTENTS

Why is our travel information the best in the world? It's simple: our authors are passionate, dedicated travellers. They don't take freebies in exchange for positive coverage so you can be sure the advice you're given is impartial. They travel widely to all the popular spots, and off the beaten track. They don't research using just the internet or phone. They discover new places not included in any other guidebook. They personally visit thousands of hotels, restaurants, palaces, trails, galleries, temples and more. They speak with dozens of locals every day to make sure you get the kind of insider knowledge only a local could tell you. They take pride in getting all the details right, and in telling it how it is. Think you can do it? Find out how at **lonelyplanet.com**.

THIS IS MARRAKESH

Within minutes of arrival in Marrakesh's Medina (Old City) you'll learn a new word: '*Balek!*' Roughly, 'Move it or lose it, donkey coming through!'

Donkey carts may not inspire the same adrenaline-rushing alertness as careening Vespas loaded with oranges, taxi drivers who mistake their Fiats for Formula 1 cars, and carpet sellers in hot pursuit of customers with their absolute last price. But once you glimpse the carts painted with good-luck symbols hurtling headlong through narrow souqs (covered market streets), you too will leap to the sidelines and watch in awe as Marrakesh rushes ahead by all available means.

Where is the city headed in such a hurry? Marrakesh has a hot date – with you actually. King Mohammed VI proclaimed that by 2020 Morocco will welcome 20 million visitors, with Marrakesh as the main point of entry. Since in a long weekend a traveller may spend about £775, or three to four months' salary for most Moroccans, every visitor is a VIP in Marrakesh. Luckily, showing guests a good time comes readily to the *bahja*, or joyous ones, as Marrakshis are known. The Djemaa el-Fna has enchanted visitors for a millennium, with its chorus of 100 chefs singing their own praises, Gnaoua musicians banging out funky freedom songs on *ginbris* (three-stringed banjos) and potion sellers' chants promising cures for rheumatism and heartbreak. Guests get the royal treatment in traditional hammams (bathhouses) and authentic riads, elegant mudbrick courtyard mansions that make the Medina a Unesco World Heritage Site.

The Pink City promises a rosier future for Moroccans – 40% of whom subsist below the poverty line – because travellers today are seeking the inspiring, culturally enriching, gourmet travel options Marrakesh has to offer. Given its 1000-year history of hospitality, a 2011 cafe bombing came as a shock to cosmopolitan Marrakesh. But after surviving historic triumphs and tragedies with its spirits and pink mudbrick walls marvelously intact, this city knew what to do. Marrakesh dried its tears, gathered its legendary wits, and put on another pot of welcoming mint tea. For up-to-date information about Morocco, see www.lonelyplanet.com/marrakesh.

Top left Painted door in the central courtyard of Musée de Marrakesh (82) **Top right** Ancient Berber symbols feature in this design at Ministero del Gusto (p103) **Bottom** One of the many colourful food stalls (p72) set up each afternoon on the Djemaa el-Fna

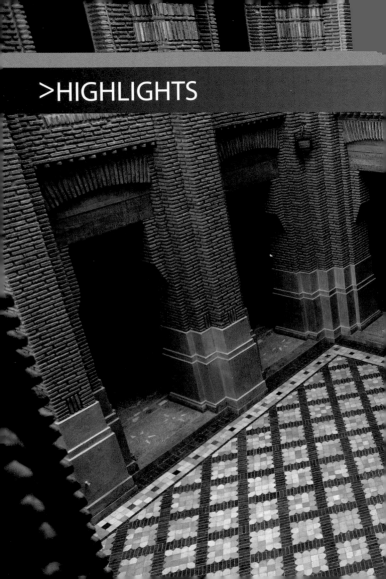

One of the rooms at the Théâtre Royal (p61) in Nouvelle Ville

>1 DJEMAA EL-FNA

WATCH NONSTOP DRAMA IN THE DJEMAA EL-FNA

PT Barnum was bluffing when he called his circus 'the greatest show on earth'; that title has belonged to the Djemaa el-Fna for almost a millennium. The hoopla and *halqa* (street theatre) has been nonstop here ever since this plaza was used for public executions in about 1050 – hence its name, which means 'assembly of the dead'.

The curtain goes up on the Djemaa el-Fna around 9am, when juice vendors haul in carts loaded with oranges, potion purveyors and henna tattoo artists set up shop under umbrellas, and pedestrians begin their dance dodging motor scooters and donkey carts. Water sellers in fringed hats lug their metal dispensers around the plaza as though they haven't heard of bottled water, gamely pausing to pose for photos for a few dirhams.

The second act begins in the afternoon, when the entertainers arrive. Snake charmers strike up oboe numbers that may sound dissonant to humans, but are apparently irresistible club tunes among the serpent set. Like all-male cheerleader squads, track-suited acrobats attempt to rouse afternoon cafe crowds with back flips and human pyramids. But Gnaoua musicians always steal the show with syncopated songs heavy on drums and castanets; working

themselves and their audience into an ecstatic trance that gets fez tassels spinning, toes tapping and everyone grinning. As always in the Djemaa, applause and tips in any amount keep the good vibes and encores coming.

When evening arrives, storytellers spellbind crowds with legends told in Arabic and dramatic gestures that need no translation. Astrologers, healers and cross-dressing belly dancers move to the periphery as some 100 food stalls set up shop and barbecue smoke rises from the Djemaa like dry ice in preparation for the evening's grande finale. The reviews are in: Unesco declared the Djemaa el-Fna a Masterpiece of World Heritage in 2001.

See also p68 and p70.

CAMEO APPEARANCES

Stick around and you might catch a command performance by special guest stars in the Djemaa:
> Scribes who will read, write and notarise Dear John letters, no questions asked.
> Dentists with pointy pliers and a jar of teeth… Enough said.
> Glass eaters, apparently here to entertain and keep the dentists in business.
> Fire swallowers who make glass and *harissa* 'hot sauce' seem digestible by comparison.

HIGHLIGHTS

>2 SOUQS

GET LOST AND FIND TREASURES IN THE SOUQS: THE ULTIMATE URBAN LABYRINTH

You haven't really been to Marrakesh until you've gotten lost in these covered markets. Slow down and look around: when rays of sunlight through the palm-frond roof illuminate a lute maker at work, you've found the Instrument-makers' Souq (Souq Kimakhine), and if you glimpse sparks flying as old bicycle parts are refashioned into lanterns, Souq Haddadine (Blacksmiths' Souq) has found you. Souq Sebbaghine (Dyers' Souq) is the most picturesque, with skeins of freshly dyed saffron and vermillion wool hung to dry against Marrakshi pink walls and Saharan blue skies.

But don't stop there; dive into the labyrinthine *qissaria* (covered market) between Souq Smata (Slipper Souq) and Souq Semmarine (Leather Souq), where artisans in cubbyhole workshops fashion next season's It Bag using tools and techniques inherited from great-great-grandparents. From morning to evening, this area buzzes with the sounds of handiwork in progress and artisans calling out greetings to passers-by in five languages. Anyone who stops by is promptly given a nickname – divulge your favourite footballer or hobby, and there you have it – and return customers are treated to warm greetings and hot tea.

Pause for unexpected beauty and banter often, because what are the chances you'll come this way again? Even locals and compass-equipped cartographers lose their way in millennia-old Medina

---

TOP FIVE SOUQ JOKES

Multilingual Marrakshi vendors make jokes of any overheard word, and no trip to the souqs would be complete without hearing one of these groaners:

> 'Berber whiskey': mint tea
> 'Air-conditioned shoes': raffia slippers
> 'Berber 4x4': donkey cart
> '30 camels': the going rate for a dowry; hold out for a Vespa
> 'Berber Adidas': rubber-soled *babouches* (slippers)

streets flanked by some 3000 *derbs* (winding alleys), which predate city planning and defy satellite mapping. You could hire a guide, but you'd be missing most of the fun and all the deals – odds are your guide is related to the shopkeeper or gets a commission. Go it alone instead, and never be too proud to bow gracefully out of a bargaining session or backtrack the way you came. Think of the souqs as the Bermuda Triangle of shopping: if you emerge blinking in the sunlight of the Djemaa el-Fna clutching fewer than five shopping bags, a victorious glass of orange juice is in order.

See also p81.

>3 ALI BEN YOUSSEF MEDERSA
**GET A HIGHER EDUCATION IN MOROCCAN ARTISTRY
AT ALI BEN YOUSSEF MEDERSA**

Insiders say Marrakesh's palaces can't compare with its wonders wrought for the glory of God. While local mosques and *zaouias* (saint shrines) are closed to non-Muslims, you can see what the insiders mean at this medersa (Quranic school). Founded in the 14th century under the Merenids, the Ali ben Youssef Medersa was once the largest in North Africa and remains one of the most splendid. Look up in the entry hall, and admire intricately carved cedar cupolas and *mashrabiyya* (wooden-lattice screen) balconies. To add an ahh to that ooh, enter the medersa's courtyard. The arcaded cloisters are Hispano-Moresque wonders of five-colour, high-lustre *zellij* (mosaic) and ingenious Iraqi-style Kufic stucco, with letters intertwined in leaves and knots. Just…wow. Or as the medersa's students might say: *Allahuakbar* (God is great).

Facing stiff competition from medersas in Fez, the school closed in 1962. But in its heyday, up to 900 students lived in the 130 dorm rooms here – and shared one bathroom. Upstairs, a 3-sq-metre dorm room overlooking the courtyard shows how students lived, with a sleeping mat, writing implements, a Quran bookstand and a hotplate. Just like your university days minus the partying, and with even more prayers come exam time.

See also p80.

>4 SAADIAN TOMBS

REVISIT MARRAKESH'S GOLDEN AGE AT SAADIAN TOMBS
Who says you can't take it with you? Surely not 16th century Saadian
Sultan Ahmed el-Mansour el-Dahbi, known as 'The Victorious' for
defeating Portuguese foes of the Sudan, and as 'The Golden' for
cheating customers with exorbitant sugar prices. With his spoils, this
Marrakshi Midas gilded the lavish stucco-and-marble Chamber of the
Twelve Pillars to make it a suitably glorious final resting place.

The sultan was quite the family man, numerically speaking, and
kept his many wives, relatives, children and servants close even in
death – hence the 170-plus tombs in this compound. The small *zellij*
tombs in the gardens are for wives, trusty Jewish councillors and
lesser relations, while the alpha-male Saadian princes are interred in
the Chamber of the Three Niches. The sultan's mother has her own
mausoleum, vigilantly guarded by stray cats in the courtyard.

El-Mansour died in splendour in 1603, but a scant few decades
later Alawite Sultan Moulay Ismail walled up the Saadian Tombs to
keep his predecessors out of sight and mind. Accessible only through
a small passage in the Kasbah Mosque, the tombs were neglected by
all except the storks until aerial photography exposed them in 1917.

See also p111.

HIGHLIGHTS

>5 KOUTOUBIA MINARET

HEAR THE KOUTOUBIA'S MELODIC MUEZZIN RISE ABOVE THE HAWKERS' HUBBUB

Five times a day, one voice rises above the Djemaa din for the adhan (call to prayer): that's the muezzin atop the Koutoubia Minaret calling the faithful in all four cardinal directions, so no Marrakshi can claim to have missed a reminder of the *salah* (five daily prayers). Other muezzin may be less than punctual, shout out a sura (Quranic verse), or clear their throats like chain smokers, but not at the Koutoubia: the entire sura flows with impeccable syllabic accents and an unbroken melody from beginning to end.

The Koutoubia Minaret is the ultimate Marrakshi muezzin gig. This 12th-century, 70m-high tower is the architectural prototype for Seville's La Giralda and Rabat's Tour Hassan, and it's a monumental cheat sheet of Moorish ornament: scalloped keystone arches, jagged merlons (crenulations) and mathematically pleasing proportions. Originally the minaret was sheathed in Marrakshi pinkish plaster, but experts opted to preserve its exposed stone and time-tested character in its 1990s restoration. The Koutoubia mosque is off limits to non-Muslims, but the gardens are fair game, and a prime location to hear the Koutoubia adhan up close.

See also p70.

>6 BAHIA PALACE

PREPARE TO BE FLOORED BY THE WOODWORKED CEILINGS AT BAHIA PALACE

Imagine what you could build with Morocco's top artisans at your service for 14 years, and here you have it. *La Bahia* (The Beautiful) boasts floor-to-ceiling decoration begun by Grand Vizier Si Moussa in the 1860s, and further embellished from 1894 to 1900 by slave-turned-vizier Abu 'Bou' Ahmed. The painted, gilded, inlaid woodwork ceilings still have the intended effect of awing crowds, while the carved stucco is cleverly slanted downward to meet the gaze. Detractors sniff that the polychrome *zellij* could be fitted together more tightly, but we'd like to see them try.

Though only a portion of the palace's 8 hectares and 150 rooms is open to the public, you can see the unfurnished, opulently ornamented harem that once housed Bou Ahmed's four wives and 24 concubines, and the grand Court of Honour, once packed with people begging for the despot's mercy. Warlord Madani Glaoui entertained European friends and tortured Moroccan enemies here from 1908 to 1911, until his French guests booted their host out and established the Protectorate's *résident-généraux*. Mohammed VI is more careful about his choice of royal guests, who range from dignitaries to rapper Sean 'Diddy' Combs.

See also p108.

>7 HAMMAMS

GET STEAM CLEANED, ROUGHED UP AND PLASTERED WITH MUD IN A TRADITIONAL HAMMAM

Slimed, roughed up, and slathered in mud: what sounds like very naughty playground behaviour is actually a glorious Moroccan spa treatment. Keeping your skin fresh and dewy this close to the Sahara requires extreme measures, and Berbers have stuck to more or less the same beauty regimen for a millennium. In a steamy domed hammam (bathhouse), a *tebbaya* (bath attendant) slathers your skin with slippery *savon noir*, black soap made with palm and olive oil plus pore-cleansing essential oils. When the going gets rough, the rough get thoroughly scrubbed with an exfoliating *kessa* (rough-textured glove). Many layers of shed dead skin later – you'll be surprised and slightly aghast to see just how much was clogging your pores – you're ready for a soothing *rhassoul* (mud scalp rub) before a fragrant orange-flower water rinse and a coating of emollient argan oil.

Does this regime actually work? Maybe too well: back in the 7th century, Ummayad caliphs took a particular shine to Berber women, and drafted many into their royal harems. So as you emerge from the hammam soft, pliable and glowing, be thankful those pesky Ummayads were driven out of Berber territory by warrior Queen al-Kahina – and don't forget to reapply your SPF30.

See also p143.

>8 JARDIN MAJORELLE

STRIKE A POSE AMID HIGH-FASHION CACTI IN YVES SAINT LAURENT'S JARDIN MAJORELLE

Some people send thank-you cards, but Yves Saint Laurent gave this spectacular garden as a token of appreciation to the city that adopted him in 1964 after a sequence of events that included, in rather unfortunate order: launching hippie fashion, fame as a ground-breaking gay icon, and an obligatory stint in the French military.

Saint Laurent and his partner Pierre Bergé bought the garden with its Art Deco villa, now the Museum of Islamic Arts, from acclaimed landscape painter Jacques Majorelle. In 1924 Majorelle comple-mented his collection of rare flora with vivid touches of colour for a look that remains shockingly contemporary: fuchsia bougainvillea explodes from Day-Glo yellow terracotta planters, cacti lean against cobalt-blue plaster walls like slouching rock stars, and goldfish flash neon orange in pale-green reflecting pools.

To best appreciate Majorelle's artistic accomplishment, visit at high noon or on a sweltering summer's day, when the place is like a desert mirage. The blue and green hues seem to quench your thirst, bamboo thickets rustle in the slightest breeze, and turtles lazing around under drawbridges set a fine example.

See also p41.

>9 DAR SI SAID

EXPLORE MOROCCAN ARTS AND FIND HOME DECOR INSPIRATION AT THE SUBLIME DAR SI SAID

Historical rumour has it that Grand Vizier 'Bou' Ahmed's brother Si Said wasn't the brightest dirham in the royal treasury, but judging by his palace, he might've been craftier than anyone suspected. While 'Bou' Ahmed demanded a rush job on the Bahia Palace, Si Said gave his *maâlems* (master craftspeople) time to refine their work. Today the Bahia is a marvel of glitz with the occasional slapdash slip, but Dar Si Said is a model of restrained 19th-century elegance. Si Said's artisans outdid themselves in the upstairs wedding chamber, covering the walls, musicians' balconies and ceiling with a truly joyous profusion of floral ornament – you can almost hear the women ululating.

The Dar Si Said also features a well-curated selection of southern Moroccan arts with like items grouped together, so visitors can appreciate Moroccan artisans' ingenious variations on kohl (eyeliner) bottles and inlaid daggers. The carved wooden doors on display are similar in style but always distinct in detail, so that you can almost imagine the family living behind each one, and the baby Ferris wheel and ancient kitchen utensils on display will give you a new appreciation of childproofing and food processors.

See also p109.

>10 MOROCCAN FEASTS

FEAST IN STYLE AT A MULTICOURSE MOROCCAN *DIFFA*

When mere dinner won't do, Moroccans celebrate with a proper *diffa* (feast). Seasonal delicacies are served family style from shared platters, and guests are cajoled into eating with a good-humoured insistence that would do your grandmother proud. In restaurants and at Moroccan weddings and family functions, the feeding frenzy is often punctuated with conversation and live musical entertainment.

The desired result is happy taste buds, harmony among humankind and the sleep of the dead. But be warned: some palace restaurants attempt to distract diners from their dismal cafeteria-style fare with laser shows, belly dancers helpfully simulating digestion and over-the-top decor straight out of a genie's bottle. Accept no imitations for the real meal deal, which includes three to five courses cooked to order and perfection, whether fixed-price or à la carte.

A daring *diffa* begins with a starter of three to seven cooked salads ranging from slow-cooked smoky eggplant to tangy-sweet beets, possibly followed by legendary Moroccan *bastilla* (pigeon pie). Next up: succulent meats barbecued, slow-roasted, and/or served dissolving into bubbling, delicate sauces flavoured with *smen* (seasoned clarified butter). Then comes fluffy conical couscous piled with seasonal vegetables and scented with saffron. Save room for dessert, which could be simple cinnamon-laced oranges or kingly *bastilla* (flaky pastry with rich cream and almonds). Afterwards, bow down to the *dada* (cook) – if you still can.

See also p134.

>11 MUSÉE DE MARRAKESH

UNCOVER PALACE INTRIGUES AMONG THE TREASURES AT MUSÉE DE MARRAKESH

If these 19th-century palace walls could talk, they'd dish out dirt on Queen Victoria and Mehdi Mnebhi, minister of defence during the brief, troubled 1894–1908 reign of Sultan Moulay Abdelaziz. While Minister Mnebhi was busy schmoozing European royals and receiving a medal from Queen Victoria, sneaky England was secretly conspiring with France and Spain to carve up North Africa. When the sultan ceded control to France and Spain, Mnebhi beat a hasty retreat to Tangiers, and Anglophile autocrat Pasha Glaoui snatched this palace. After Independence, it was seized by the state and became Marrakesh's first girls' school in 1965.

Today the pristine palace is a haven of serenity, elegantly restored by the Omar Benjelloun Foundation. The arcaded inner courtyard is flanked by traditional arts displays, including recent travelling shows of High Atlas carpets and Moroccan Jewish artefacts. Also of interest is the original hammam, with several chambers to accommodate varying needs for heat, from the vaguely arthritic to the seriously hung-over. But there's still plenty of fodder for controversy in the lovely green and white *douira* gallery, which exhibits highly variable modern art ranging from cool Pakistani pop-art miniatures to kitschy Italian clown paintings.

See also p82.

>MARRAKESH DIARY

You'll never need an excuse for a party in the home of the *bahja* (joyous ones). Join a Gnaoua *leila* (trance jam session) any night in the Djemaa el-Fna, where cross-dressing belly dancers invite partners with playful flicks of their veils. Lately savvy club promoters have organised shindigs in other outdoor venues, including lounge music with Bryan Ferry at the Badi Palace (www.purodesert lounge.com). Official occasions such as the annual film festival or marathon find listings in French at www.marrakechpocket.com and www.maghrebarts ma) are inevitably upstaged by raucous sing-along Bollywood screenings and children cheering themselves hoarse for hometown favourite runners.

Entry to the Ali ben Youssef Medersa (p80), a centre of Quranic learning in the 14th century

JANUARY

Marathon of Marrakesh

www.marathon-marrakech.com

Run like there's a carpet seller after you from the Djemaa to the Palmeraie and back.

FEBRUARY

MadJazz

www.madjazz-festival.com

Marrakesh invents new sounds nightly with Gnawa castanets, jazz riffs and Jimi Hendrix guitar licks.

Marrakesh marathon training in the Palmeraie

APRIL

Aicha des Gazelles

www.rallyeaichadesgazelles.com

This gazelle will run you down: women race off-road through the Sahara to Essaouira.

Jardin'Art Garden Festival

www.jardinsdumaroc.com/festival

The Pink City goes green with living sculptures, sustainability forums and Cyberpark concerts on the second weekend in April.

Essaouira Alizés (Trade Winds) Classical Music Festival

www.alizesfestival.com

The third weekend in April sees 20 concerts in four days, with interfaith chants, original compositions and Mozart megahits.

JUNE

Essaouira Gnaoua Music Festival

www.festival-gnaoua.net

Surfers, Sufis, Moroccan Rastas and roots musicologists get funky with Gnaoua and pan-African music at North Africa's grooviest music festival on the third weekend in June.

JULY

Marrakesh Festival of Popular Arts

www.marrakechfestival.com

The only thing hotter than Marrakesh in July is this free-form folk fest held on the

Gnaoua musicians performing in Djemaa el-Fna (p70)

first weekend in July. Berber musicians, dancers and street performers from around the country pour into Marrakesh to thrill the masses, with impromptu performance marathons in the Djemaa that easily rival officially scheduled international folk acts.

SEPTEMBER

Imilchil Marriage Festival

Intense flirting and negotiation ensue at this Middle Atlas *moussem* (celebration),

where women come from miles around to harvest husbands. Date depends on harvest schedule.

OCTOBER

Marrakesh International Art Fair

www.marrakechartfair.com

Fifty art openings are rolled into one at this pan-Mediterranean contemporary art showcase.

DECEMBER

Marrakesh International Film Festival

http://en.festivalmarrakech.info

Sundance seems staid compared with this eclectic showcase of independent and postcolonial film that includes movies shot in Morocco. Hollywood glitterati such as Milos Forman, Sigourney Weaver and 2010 jury president John Malkovich are overshadowed by literal red-carpet royalty and raucous Bollywood screenings in the Djemaa. On the first or second weekend in December.

PUBLIC HOLIDAYS

While state holidays are held on the same date each year, the dates of religious holidays change each year in accordance with the lunar Hejira calendar. See p164 for a list of public holiday dates for 2012, 2013 and 2014.

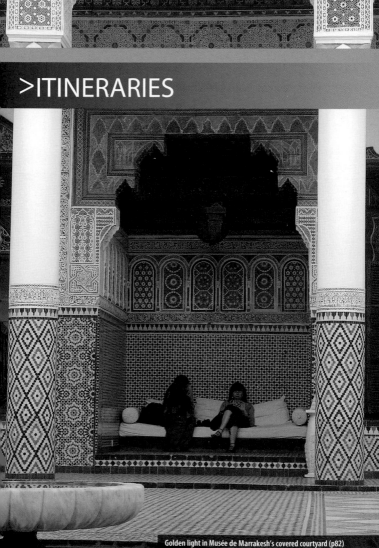

Golden light in Musée de Marrakesh's covered courtyard (p82)

ITINERARIES

DAY ONE

Get juiced on freshly squeezed OJ in the Djemaa el-Fna (p70) and rush headlong into the souqs along Rue el-Mouassine, past Souq Sebbaghine (Dyers' Souq) toward Rahba Kedima (p83) and herbalists' special offers of 'Berber Viagara' (galanga). Compare wares you've seen in the souqs with examples of prime craftsmanship at the Musée de Marrakesh (p82), and see how your alma mater stacks up against the glorious Ali ben Youssef Medersa (p80). Follow 150 years of Moroccan photography with home-cooked tagines on the rooftop of Maison de la Photographie (p82) or feast in style at Le Foundouk (p88). Dodge a dozen carpet sellers on your way back to the Djemaa and congratulations: you've got the hang of Marrakesh.

DAY TWO

Your Marrakshi romance begins at Dar Si Said (p109), where the exuber-antly painted wedding chamber may inspire ululation. Down Riad Zitoun el-Jedid, the bodaciously ornamented Bahia Palace (p108) harem may make you rethink both decor and monogamy. For lunch, enjoy a tagine hot off the burner in Restaurant Place des Ferblantiers (p114) then sip beer or wine amid the storks' nests atop Kosybar (p115). Peek into the Badi Palace (p108) for storks' love nests and the miraculous marquetry of the Koutoubia Minbar (p109), then pay your respects to the sultan who left his wives out in the rain at the Saadian Tombs (p111). Unwind in the steamy Sultana Spa (p116) or with a hammam and massage for two at Le Bain Bleu (p105), and let Marrakesh work its charms.

LAZY DAY

Roll out of your riad around noon and grab a taxi to Jardin Majorelle (p41), where towering cacti and vibrant colours awaken the senses. Take a taxi to a late lunch at Al Fassia (p48), then hit the gallery scene along Rue de Yougoslavie en route to Rue de la Liberté for boutique-browsing and cap-puccino at mod Kechmara (p59). Mosey down Ave Mohammed V to watch artisans at work at Ensemble Artisanal (p40), and stop to smell the roses and send insincere 'wish you were here' emails to coworkers at Cyberpark

---

Top left The Koutoubia Mosque and gardens (p70) **Top right** Bahia Palace (p108)
Bottom Artisans at work at Ensemble Artisanal (p40)

(p37). Dinner at La Table du Marché (p52) is only a couple of blocks from drinks at Jad Mahal (p58) and groovy DJs at Le Comptoir (p55).

HOT SUMMER DAY
Take your cue from the empty streets and get out of town. Take a mountain-stream hike in cool, picturesque Imlil (p146) then stop at Dar Taliba (see boxed text, p157) for a refreshing Berber tea and a visit to the nonprofit herb garden and school (donations appreciated and used wisely). Or take a cooking class in the Palmeraie at Jnane Tamsna (p64). If you can't stand the heat, you can get out of the kitchen and dive into one of four pools amid organic gardens – and fight global warming by donating to a palm-tree-planting program (see boxed text, p157).

DURING RAMADAN
Early risers carbo-load before dawn with the faithful, then stock up on lunch supplies in the early-morning rush on the souqs or the Marché Municipale (p46). Hit the sights before returning to the riad for a nap and discreet lunch. Slackers can sleep late without missing much, and eat in at the riad before an afternoon photo safari in atmospherically deserted

When the sun sets, fasting for Ramadan ends with a feast of dates in the souqs

FORWARD PLANNING

Three weeks before you go Make riad reservations (p117), book classes in Moroccan cooking or crafts (see boxed text, p66) and trekking excursions in the High Atlas – your riad can probably do it for you – and start mastering Moroccan Arabic pleasantries for smiles and sweet deals in the souqs (see boxed text, p82).

One week before you go Book a hammam (p143) and tune into Moroccan radio online at www.maroc.net/rc to loosen up those hips. Organise a *diffa* (feast; p21) to work off on the dance floor.

The day before you go Check out what the Moroccan blogosphere's a-Twitter about at http://globalvoicesonline.org/-/world/middle-east-north-africa/morocco/ and gain insights from Moroccan author/blogger Laila Lalami at http://lailalalami.com/c/all-things-moroc can/. Start working up an appetite now for your feast – a half marathon should do the trick.

streets and monuments. Near dusk the buzz in the souqs is palpable, as dates, *harira* (lentil soup) and *chebbakia* (honey pastry) are readied for the *iftar* (break-fast) rush. At sundown the feasting begins, and when the main meal is served around 10pm, kids amped on sweets have the run of the streets and the Djemaa (p70) is packed with revellers. *Ramadan Mubarak!* (Happy Ramadan!)

FOR FREE

Breakfast is complimentary at most riads, so fuel up before you brave the souqs, where you'll be assured constantly that 'looking is free' by vendors parading temptations before you. Check out art shows at Dar Chérifa (p98) and Dar Bellarj (p80) and swing by the Mouassine Fountain (p99), where neighbourhood gossip flows freely, and *fondouqs* (p98) for glimpses of artisans at work. Ensemble Artisanal (p40) offers a closer look at crafts without the sales pressure before you hit the contemporary Moroccan art circuit at Galerie Rê (p40), Gallerie Noir Sur Blanc (p40) and Matisse Art Gallery (p41). Festivals mean free street entertainment and unbeatable people-watching – but you can always get free and funky in the Djemaa (p70) with Gnaoua musicians, whose winsome ways may convince you to part with cash for tips.

>NEIGHBOURHOODS

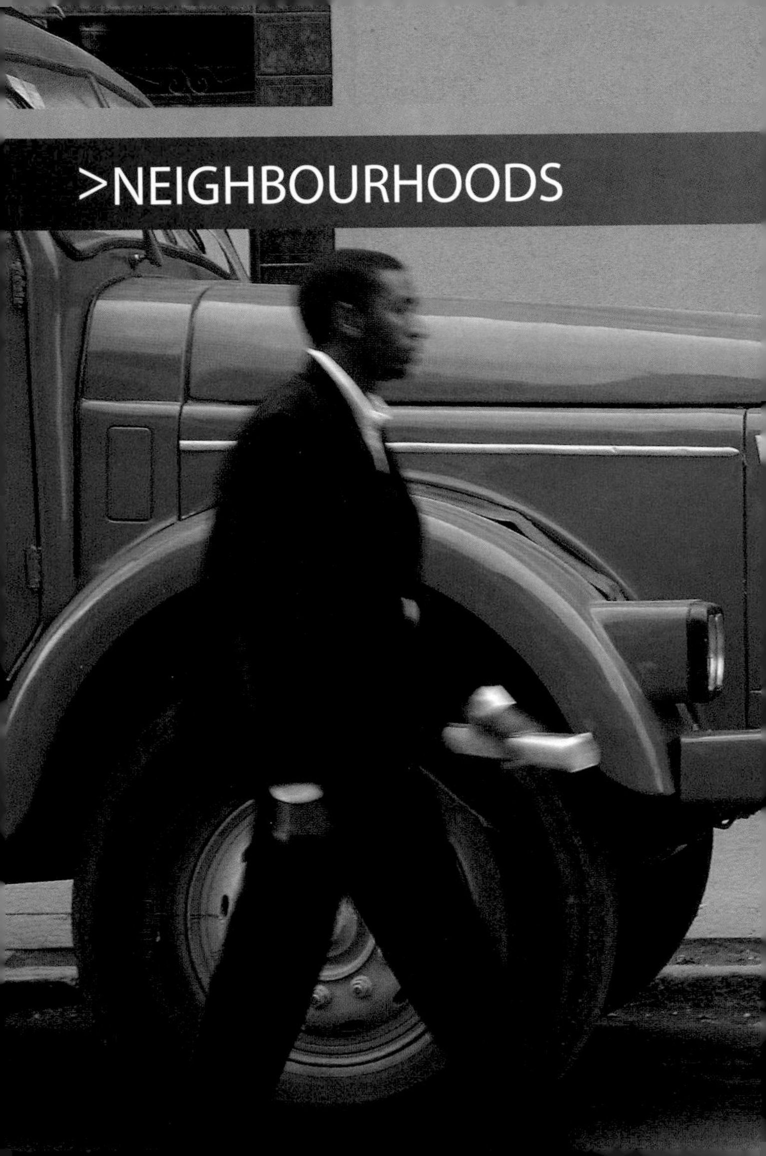

Past meets future: welcome to Marrakesh

NEIGHBOURHOODS

Urban legends have been made in Marrakesh for a millennium. Nights of decadence and music once left Nouvelle Ville hotel floors littered with Rolling Stones and Beatles and parts of Led Zeppelin.

Writers and Bohemians headed to the Medina for enlightenment and *kif* (hashish), coming away with inspiration for books such as *Hideous Kinky* and *Naked Lunch*. Today, you might visit Yves Saint Laurent's Nouvelle Ville villa, bump into Paul McCartney in the Palmeraie, eat with Jamie Oliver in the Djemaa el-Fna or meet Kate Moss, Iman or Naomi Campbell scouring the souqs for kaftans. Even Marrakesh's ancient monuments stay current: yes, that was Brangelina sipping mint tea in the Djemaa, Bryan Ferry introducing Badi Palace storks to lounge music, and rapper Sean 'Diddy' Combs dining with Mohammed VI at the Bahia Palace.

Travellers' tales usually revolve around the Djemaa el-Fna, which serves as a stage for a Unesco-honoured ensemble of storytellers, cross-dressing belly dancers, snake charmers and potion sellers. On the north side of the Djemaa el-Fna, souq traders beckon with siren calls of 'Come in… just look…some tea?' East is Derb Debachi, a labyrinth of *derbs* (winding alleys). To the west is the venerable Mouassine, with its stately riads (mudbrick courtyard mansions). North is Bab Doukkala and Dar el-Bacha, once home to Marrakesh's dreaded despot but now a friendly neighbourhood of riads, hammams and a bustling food souq. Meanwhile, south of the Djemaa el-Fna lie the Riads Zitoun, lined with artisans' showplaces and spectacular palaces. Holding down the fort further south is the royal Kasbah, containing the king's official palace and the Saadian Tombs.

The plot thickens in the Nouvelle Ville (New City), created in 1912 for French colonial elites and now a prime spot to mingle with chic Marrakshis at sidewalk cafes, Art Deco villa restaurants and local designer boutiques. The most happening Nouvelle Ville nightclubs and bars are in Guéliz (north of the Medina) and the swanky hotels of Hivernage (west of the Medina). The stylish latecomer to the Marrakesh party is Palmeraie, the nouveau-riche oasis and celebrity haunt 5km east of town.

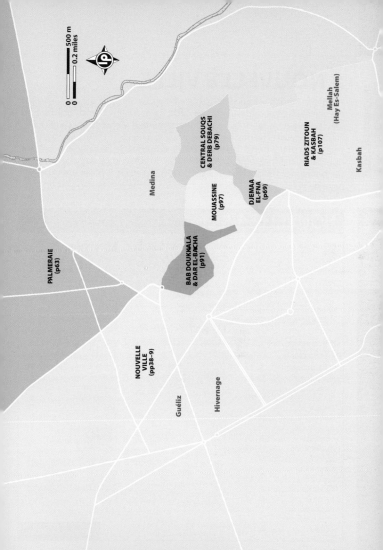

500 m
0.2 miles

PALMERAIE
(p63)

Medina

CENTRAL SOUQS
& DERB DEBACHI
(p79)

MOUASSINE
(p97)

BAB DOUKKALA
& DAR EL-BACHA
(p91)

DJEMAA
EL-FNA
(p69)

RIADS ZITOUN
& KASBAH
(p107)

Mellah
(Hay Es-Salem)

Kasbah

NOUVELLE
VILLE
(pp38-9)

Guéliz

Hivernage

> NOUVELLE VILLE

When the French set up shop in their 'New City' in 1912, they brought all the comforts of home: wide boulevards, garden villas, French bistros, and inescapable roundabouts. Independent-minded Moroccans kicked the French colonial government to the boulevard kerb in 1956, but wisely kept a few of the better bistros – and, less prudently, retained the baffling roundabouts. More radical changes have occurred in recent years, with the boom in travel and a new Marrakshi middle class. Hivernage villas have been replaced by fancy hotels and, with the outstanding exception

NOUVELLE VILLE

🔘 SEE
Cyberpark 1 F5
David Bloch Gallery 2 C7
Galerie Noir Sur Blanc 3 A8
Galerie Photo 127 ....4 C8
Galerie Rê 5 D3
Jardin Majorelle 6 E1
Matisse Art Gallery 7 A8

🏠 SHOP
Acima Supermarket 8 A2
ACR Librairie d'Art 9 B7
African Lodge 10 D3
Alrazal 11 D3
Ben Rahal Carpets 12 B8
Côté Sud 13 B8
Couleurs Primaires 14 A7
Kaftan Queen
  Boutique 15 C3
L'Atelier du Vin 16 E3
Les Parfums du Soleil ...17 C2
Librairie Chatr 18 B2
Linéaire B Cosmetics 19 C2
L'Orientaliste 20 B8
Maison Rouge 21 B8
Manufacture de
  Vêtements pour
  Enfants Sages 22 B7

Marché Municipale 23 E3
Michéle Baconnier 24 B7
Moor 25 B7
Newstand Marché
  Municipale ....(see 23)
Scénes de Lin 26 D3
Yahya 27 A8

🍽 EAT
Al Fassia 28 B7
Alizia 29 E6
Amaia 30 C4
Amandine 31 B4
Azar 32 C4
Café 16 ....33 D4
Catanzaro 34 D3
Dino 35 E4
La Table du Marché 36 F7
L'Annexe 37 C2
Le Chat Qui Rit 38 C4
Le Grande Café de
  la Poste 39 D4
Marché Central 40 E3
Pâtisserie Adamo 41 D3
Pâtisserie al-Jawda 42 C4
Samak al Bahria 43 C4

🍸 DRINK
Bab Hotel Pool
  Lounge & Skybar 44 B3
Café des Négociants 45 A7
Coffee Marrak' Chic 46 E4
Le Comptoir 47 F7
Le Melting Pot 48 A8
Yellow Submarine 49 B4

⭐ PLAY
Actions Sports Loisirs ..50 F1
Cinéma Colisée 51 B3
Institut Français 52 A2
Jardin Harti 53 D5
Kawkab Jeux 54 D3
Kechmara 55 B8
La Casa 56 D8
Le Diamant Noir 57 E4
Le Théâtro 58 E7
Les Secrets de
  Marrakesh 59 C3
Lotus Club 60 E6
Royal Tennis Club 61 D5
Théâtre Royal 62 B5

Please see over for map

Hanging out in Cyberpark (below)

of the Jardin Majorelle and Guéliz, gardens have been mostly filled in with townhouses and apartments. But it's hard to bemoan such bygone glories, especially with your mouth full at tasty new Nouvelle Ville restaurants and patisseries. Sleeping seems overrated in hot spot–filled Hivernage, fuelled with espresso from Guéliz cafes. And in the past decade, the imported culture of Guéliz has been upgraded with home-grown galleries and boutiques showcasing Moroccan artists and designers, a grand royal theatre and a literary cafe. The Nouvelle Ville never looked so new.

SEE
CYBERPARK
Ave Mohammed V, near Bab Nkob;
free wi-fi & internet kiosks, indoor

computer use Dh10/hr; 🕑 **9am-7pm;**
Tiptoe through the tulips to check email at the Cyberpark, an 8-hectare royal garden dating

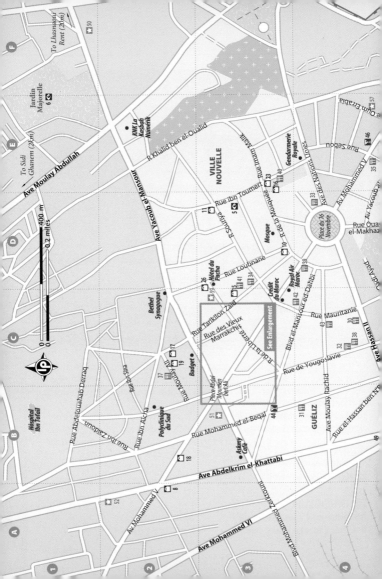

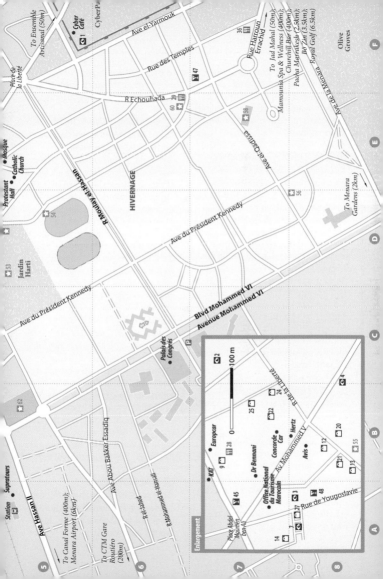

from about 1700 that now offers free wi-fi. The paths are lined with orange trees, palms and internet kiosks – wait your turn on benches filled with teenagers and nervous online daters.

◉ DAVID BLOCH GALLERY
☎ 0524 457595; 8 bis Rue des Vieux Marrakchis; www.davidblochgallery.com; ⏱ 10.30am-1.30pm & 3.30-7.30pm Tue-Sat, 3.30-7.30 Mon

Artists from both sides of the Mediterranean explore the fine line between traditional calligraphy and urban graffiti. A recent show featured mounted camel-head trophies designed by Younes Duret, and reimagined by graphic artists: Morran ben Lahcen covered one camel's head with molten vinyl LPs, French graffiti artist O'Clock turned another into a unicorn, while Mohamed Melehi defaced/refaced his with lipstick.

◉ ENSEMBLE ARTISANAL
Ave Mohammed V, opposite Cyberpark; admission free; ⏱ 9.30am-12.30pm & 3-7pm Mon-Sat; ♿ ⚤

Answers to your every 'how'd they make that?' are on display at this state-run artisans complex. Ringing the courtyard are set-price boutiques that give you a benchmark for the maximum you should pay for handmade brass tea trays and felt beanies in the souqs, and

to the right are bigger workshops where you can watch carpets, baskets and handbags being made.

◉ GALERIE NOIR SUR BLANC
☎ 0524 422416; 48 Rue de Yougoslavie; ⏱ 10am-1pm & 3-7pm Mon-Sat

Get in on the ground floor of the Moroccan contemporary art boom at this 1st-floor showcase of major Moroccan talent. A recent show featured elemental calligraphic paintings by Marrakshi Larbi Cherkaoui, whose words break free of the page and seem to turn backflips on canvas. Friendly, well-informed staff provide useful insights about recurring motifs and fresh ideas in Moroccan art.

◉ GALERIE PHOTO 127
☎ 0524 432667; 2nd fl, 127 Ave Mohammed V; ⏱ 11am-7pm Tue-Sat

Like any worthwhile Chelsea gallery, this one is up a dim, once-grand staircase and in an industrial-chic chamber with the obligatory exposed brick-and-concrete wall. Shows vary from straightforward travel photography to more interpretive works, mostly by Mediterranean artists.

◉ GALERIE RÊ
☎ 0524 432258; www.galeriere.com; Résidence Al Andalous III, cnr Rue de la Mosquée & Rue Ibn Toumert; ⏱ 10am-1pm & 3-8pm Mon-Sat

A slick, two-storey showplace featuring emerging Moroccan artists and Mediterranean artists with connections to Morocco. Standouts include the rough-edged minimalist paintings of M'barek Bouhchichi and molten sculptures by Marrakshi Touria Othman. Openings offer instant immersion in Marrakesh's eclectic creative set of paint-stained hipsters and Bohemian billionaires.

◎ JARDIN MAJORELLE
☎ 0524 301852; cnr Ave Yacoub el-Mansour & Ave Moulay Abdullah; garden Dh30, museum Dh15; ☯ 8am-6pm summer, 8am-5.30pm winter ✗ ♿ ⚐

Not your grandma's garden, unless your grandma was a fashion icon. Landscape painter Jacques Majorelle created this splashy lemon yellow, cobalt blue and cool green modern art retreat in 1924. Yves Saint Laurent bought it with his partner Pierre Bergé, entrusting it to the city of Marrakesh upon his passing. The Art Deco villa is now the Museum of Islamic Arts, which houses Saint Laurent's collection of decorative arts plus Majorelle's elegant lithographs of Southern Moroccan scenery. A new cafe on the premises offers drinks and fresh lunches at high-fashion prices, but you can't argue with the view. See p19 for more.

◎ MATISSE ART GALLERY
☎ 0524 448326; www.matisse-art-gallery.com; 43 Passage Ghandouri, off 61 Rue de Yougoslavie; ☯ 9am-5pm

Polished describes this marble-fronted gallery and the contemporary Moroccan artworks it showcases. Farid Belkahia's organically shaped henna paintings evoke Berber blessings and ancient landscape formations, and you can't miss works by Marrakesh's most famous artist, Mahi Binebine. His haloed figures in natural local pigments and beeswax are tinged with melancholy, like the imprint of a loved one who's just left the room. Vintage Orientalist works are tucked away on the mezzanine, and charming gallerists will show you a treasure trove of larger contemporary works through a trap door.

◎ MENARA GARDENS
Ave de la Menara; garden admission free, picnic pavilion Dh20; ☯ 5.30am-6.30pm

Local lore tells of a sultan who seduced guests over dinner, then lovingly chucked them in the Menara Gardens' reflecting pools to drown. But nowadays dunking seems the furthest thing from the minds of couples canoodling poolside amid these royal olive groves. Clear days bring families for picnics in a stately 19th-century pavillion, dromedary rides near the park entry, and photo-ops against the High Atlas mountain backdrop. If you stay for sunset, stick to paths to leave couples their privacy.

🛍 SHOP

🏠 ACIMA SUPERMARKET *Food*
☎ 0524 430453; 109 Ave Abdelkrim el-Khattabi, Guéliz & cnr Ave Yacoub el-Mansour, near Jardin Majorelle, Guéliz; 🕑 8.30am-11pm
When you're homesick for modern convenience, here you have it: all the picnic fixings and trekking snacks you could want, when you want them, in an air-conditioned, tidy supermarket. Offers a vast selection of foods, household goods, wine and beer.

🏠 ACR LIBRAIRIE D'ART *Books*
☎ 0524 446792; www.acr-edition.com; 55 Blvd Mohammed Zerktouni, Guéliz; 🕑 9am-12.30pm & 3-7pm Mon-Sat
Marrakesh's best selection of coffee-table (or would that be mint tea–table?) books, including handsome ones on Moroccan arts and architecture, cookbooks, and how-to guides on *tadelakt* (polished plaster), *zellij* (mosaic) and other local crafts. Most are produced by Arab-French publisher ACR Editions, but there are some locally published and English-language books too. Ask

the savvy staff about upcoming art openings, and local artists who offer classes. The shop is at the end of a pedestrian passageway.

🏠 AFRICAN LODGE
Housewares
☎ 0524 439584; 1 Rue Loubnan; 🕑 10am-1pm & 3.30-8pm Mon-Sat
Before you hanker after camel-saddle coffee tables and henna-painted orb table lamps at this ultramod African design showcase, look into shipping at the DHL office around the corner. The Saarinen-style egg chair made out of a repurposed Libya Oil barrel is surprisingly comfortable and resists rust even in English weather, and is certain to make design aficionados curse carry-on restrictions.

🏠 ALRAZAL
Children's & Women's Fashion
☎ 0524 437884; www.alrazal.com; 55 Rue Sourya; 🕑 9.30am-1pm & 3.30-7.30pm Mon-Sat; ♿
No abracadabra is necessary to turn little ones into a fairy-tale prince or princess: a handmade, embroidered outfit from Alrazal should do the trick. For the price of what you'd pay for off-the-rack back home, you can get kiddie couture dresses and swashbuckling velvet pant sets – and yes, those silk tunics come in women's

sizes right upstairs. Alterations and made-to-measure are also possible.

🏠 BEN RAHAL CARPETS
Carpets
☎ 0524 433273; 28 Rue de la Liberté; 🕐 9am-1pm & 3-8pm Mon-Sat
For quality carpets without the usual rounds of mint tea, haggling and ceremonious hoopla, ditch the Medina and head for the fixed prices and easygoing attitudes of Ben Rahal. Don't be fooled by the size of the place: the small, careful selection may leave you spoiled for choice. Get informed about antique Berber rugs and realistic carpet prices here first, and avoid buyer's remorse in the souqs later.

🏠 CÔTÉ SUD *Housewares*
☎ 0524 438448; 4 Rue de la Liberté; 🕐 9am-1pm & 3.30-7.30pm Mon-Sat
The best-priced of the design shops along Rue de la Liberté, and the friendliest too. Downstairs, you'll discover hand-painted tea glasses, red glass chandeliers and tasselled table linens. Upstairs, you'll feel a powerful temptation to throw yourself into the embankments of pillows in white cotton cases gone wild with embroidered red flowers.

🏠 COULEURS PRIMAIRES
Art Supplies
☎ 0524 446720; 37 Passage Ghandouri, off Rue de Yougoslavie; 🕐 9.30am-1pm & 3.30-7.30pm Mon-Sat
Why let Matisse hog all the glory for painting vacations in Morocco? Find your inspiration in the streets of Marrakesh, and your raw materials at Couleurs Primaires. If you think impasto sounds like something you'd have for dinner, you can find a teacher here too. Chat up the staff and they'll hook you up with artist studio visits and Arabic calligraphy lessons.

🏠 KAFTAN QUEEN BOUTIQUE
Fashion
☎ 0661 308467; www.kaftanqueen morocco.com; 44 Rue Tarik ibn Zaid; 🕐 10am-1pm & 3.30-6.30pm Mon-Sat
Work that mod Marrakesh look with chic jersey tunics with hand-knotted silk buttons, filagree-buckled belts and disco-ready kaftans in vintage '70s prints. Snap up a dress for the price of a T-shirt back home, and be the toast of cocktail hour at Kechmara around the corner. The shop is in the entryway of Hotel Toulousain.

🏠 L'ATELIER DU VIN *Wine*
☎ 0524 457112; 87 Rue Mohamed el-Beqal; 🕐 9.30am-1pm & 3.30-8pm Tue-Thu & Sat, 2.30-8pm Mon, 9.30-12.30 & 3.30-8pm Fri

NEIGHBOURHOODS

NOUVELLE VILLE

For imported and Moroccan wines at realistic prices, follow the steady stream of riad owners to this well-stocked wine shop. In addition to a wide range of French, Italian, Spanish and Portuguese wines, they stock venerable Volubilis reds, crisp Essaouira whites, Atlantic coastal *vin gris*, and the well-priced Ferme Rouge line of old-vine reds, citrusy whites and summery rosés from Rabati vineyards. Check the store's Facebook page for upcoming wine-tasting events.

LES PARFUMS DU SOLEIL
Perfume
☎ 0524 422627; www.lesparfumsdu soleil.com; Rue Tarik ibn Ziad; ⏰ 10am-1pm & 3.30-7.30pm Mon-Sat

Those tantalising Marrakshi garden scents have been blended and bottled by ethnobotanist Abderrazzak Benchaabane, whose fragrances are drawn from native flora and inspired by Berber aromatherapy principles. 'Soir de Marrakesh' is a sultry stroll through a night-blooming garden, while 'Mogador' brings

Looking sharp in the Nouvelle Ville

a coastal breeze with traces of argan oil, Kaffir lime and cedar. 'Festival' is pure head-turning, red-carpet glamour, and no wonder: Benchaabane created it in honour of the Marrakesh International Film Festival.

☐ LIBRAIRIE CHATR *Books*
☎ 0524 447997; 19-21 Ave Mohammed V, Guéliz; ⏲ 8.30am-1pm & 3-8pm Mon-Fri, 8.30am-1pm & 4-8pm Sat
Where else can you learn about the medicinal plants of Morocco while waiting in line to buy postcards, office supplies and evocative little etchings of Medina doors? A reliable source for poolside paperbacks and Somerset Maugham classics in English, hiking maps, French and Berber language dictionaries, kids' picture books and inexpensive cookery books.

☐ LINÉAIRE B COSMETICS
Beauty Products
☎ 0524 433469; www.lineaire-b.com; 13 Rue Moulay Ali; ⏲ 9am-1pm & 3-7pm Mon-Sat
Flowery descriptions in French effusively promise therapeutic effects from organic local ingredients and superconcentrated essential oils here. Basics such as *savon noir* (black soap) cost three times what they might in the Rahba Kedima, but the speciality

items are worth the premium: rich argan oil balm scented with jasmine, after-sun lotion with Barbary figs and healing herbs, facial masks with white mud from Fez and geranium-flower essence.

☐ L'ORIENTALISTE
Housewares
☎ 0524 434074; 11 & 15 Rue de la Liberté; ⏲ 10am-1.30pm & 3.30-7pm Mon-Sat
The eternal European fascination with the other side of the Mediterranean is encouraged by this boutique, packed to overflowing with enough Arabesque accessories to equip your own harem: a Deco-decadent tea service, vintage lithographs, chip-carved ebony frames and L'Orientaliste's signature fragrances in amber, jasmine and mimosa.

☐ MAISON ROUGE *Housewares*
☎ 0524 448130; 6 Rue de la Liberté; ⏲ 9.30am-1.30pm & 3-7pm Mon-Sat
Gifts here aren't only thoughtful but clever, with sly Marrakshi wit: handbags made of vintage silk scarves, plush bath towels with hand-knotted red pompoms, collaged clutches with Moroccan teapots and sand dunes that say 'Tea in the Sahara'. Given a week, they'll stitch fine linen runners or tablecloths with the design and colours of your choosing.

NEIGHBOURHOODS

NOUVELLE VILLE

▢ MANUFACTURE DE VÊTE-MENTS POUR ENFANTS SAGES
Children's Fashion
☎ 0524 446704; 44 Rue des Vieux Marrakchis; ◷ 9am-1pm & 3.30-7pm Mon-Sat

Though the name sounds like Maoist puppet theatre ('Production of clothing for wise children') this Marrakshi children's store sells locally made kids' togs in soft, colourfully striped jersey at down-to-earth prices. While parents studiously browse the racks of child-prodigy fashion, toddlers gleefully pillage racks of polka-dotted camels and candy-striped donkeys, choosing their own rewards for good behaviour back at the riad. Wise children, indeed.

▢ MARCHÉ MUNICIPALE *Food*
Rue ibn Toumert, off Ave des Nations Unies; ◷ 8am-7pm

This pleasant, tidy covered market does a brisk trade in all the Marrakesh essentials: preserved lemons, spices, cooking tagines and, oddly enough, tennis wear. The butchers have been relegated to the south end of the market, so you don't have to contemplate horse meat when you're in the market for roses and designer knock-off T-shirts with nonsensical slogans such as 'Dior is my home'.

▢ MICHÉLE BACONNIER
Fashion
☎ 0524 449178; 12 Rue des Vieux Marrakchis; ◷ 9.30am-1.30pm & 3-7pm Mon-Sat

Marrakesh is not the place to act sartorially shy, and Michée Baconnier is determined to see you step out in fuchsia raw-silk tunics, waist-length strands of green tourmaline, boots embroidered with spiralling Berber *lugnâa* (headscarf) patterns, and Nehru-collared jackets of vintage striped silk that could be costumes from some long-lost Beatles movie in Marrakesh.

▢ MOOR *Fashion*
☎ 0524 458274; www.akbardelights.com; 7 Rue des Vieux Marrakchis; ◷ 10am-1pm & 3-7pm Tue-Sat, 3-7pm Mon, 10am-1pm Fri

Style in Marrakesh is usually tailor-made, but here couture is served hot right off the rack. As you might deduce from the cloud of white-painted tin lamps dangling overhead and wall of vintage wood calligraphy tablets, Moor specialises in sleek, minimalist designs with time-honoured Marrakshi handiwork – think Jil Sander hits the souqs. Hand-knotted silk buttons close sage-green wool coats, white *zellij* (mosaic) patterns embellish natural linen sundresses, and black cotton tunics are

NEIGHBOURHOODS

NOUVELLE VILLE

embroidered with white Moorish arches.

◻ NEWSTAND MARCHÉ MUNICIPALE *News & Magazines*
26 Marché Municipale; ⏰ 9am-7pm Mon-Sat, 9am-noon Sun
News junkies can get their fix of major English-language newspapers only a day behind, and fashionistas can take Moroccan decor ideas home with armloads of design magazines.

◻ SCE'NES DE LIN *Housewares*
☎ 0524 436108; www.scenes-de-lin.com; 70 Rue de la Liberté; ⏰ 9.30am-1.30pm & 3-7pm Mon-Sat
The urge to reupholster everything you own is an understandable urge upon entering this showcase of modern Marrakshi linens. Everything but the kitchen sink comes swathed in linen and heavyweight cotton, embroidered in arabesques, edged in tiny silk knots and/or tasselled on the corners – duvets, napkins, bathrobes, pillows – and if you really need your kitchen sink done, ask about their custom services.

◻ SIDI GHANEM *Factory Outlets*
Rte de Safi; ⏰ most outlets 9am-6pm Mon-Fri & 9am-noon Sat
The industrial quarter 4km outside Marrakesh along the Route de Safi is chock full of made-for-export design studios selling direct from their outlets. For an adventure in modern Moroccan design, hire a taxi for a couple of hours in the morning or late afternoon and troll the lanes to see what's open (hours are erratic). Score a map of the quarter at any big studio, and follow your design bliss: head to Le Magasin General for retro-styled, luxury handmade housewares; ZidZid Kids for hand-embroidered toy dromedaries; and Atelier Nihal for handwoven leather handbags and floor mats.

◻ YAHYA *Lighting*
☎ 0524 422776; www.yahyacreation.com; 61 Rue de Yougoslavie, No 49 Passage Ghandouri, Guéliz; ⏰ 9.30am-1pm & 3.30-7.30pm Mon-Thu & Sat, 9.30am-1pm Fri
These fabulous filigree lamps take the play of light to the next level: flip the switch and beams of light wink and flirt all around the room. Pity those geometric chandeliers aren't more portable, but the lozenge-shaped wall sconces and egg-shaped table lanterns add instant intrigue to dark corners. Shipping can be arranged, but insurance from Morocco isn't yet available from most shipping services – better to buy a bag and carry it on.

EAT

AL FASSIA
Moroccan à la Carte $$
☎ 0524 434060; www.alfassia-aguedal.com; 55 Blvd Mohammed Zerktouni, Guéliz & MH 9 Bis, Route de l'Ourika, Zone Touristique de l'Aguedal; ⏱ noon-10.30pm Wed-Sun; ♿

Thank goodness Al Fassia is à la carte, if only to save gourmets from our own gluttony. The array of nine starters alone is a proper feast, with orange-flower water and wild herbs raising even the lowly carrot to a crowning achievement. But there's no resisting the legendary mains, cooked Middle Atlas style by an all-women team who present the dishes with a heartfelt *b'saha* (to your health). The generous helpings seem impossible to finish, but look around and you'll see glassy-eyed diners valiantly gripping morsels of bread, scraping the last savoury caramelised onion from what was once a Berber pumpkin and lamb tagine. The seasonal menu offers enough delights for two lifetimes, but dauntless diners can call ahead to order slow-cooked lamb shoulder for two, which takes a day to prepare – enough time for you to get good and hungry.

ALIZIA *Mediterranean* $$
☎ 0524 438360; Rue Echouhada, cnr Ave Chawki; ⏱ 7pm-midnight

Al fresco dining that's sort of French, sort of Italian, and quintessentially Marrakshi. Good food and even better people-watching: in one corner of the garden, local internet daters attempt to impress one another, while in another chic Moroccan girlfriends out of a long-lost Marrakesh episode of *Sex in the City* dish over dinner and drinks.

AMAIA *Sandwiches, Snacks* $
☎ 0524 457181; 84 Ave Hassan II; ⏱ 10am-midnight Mon-Sat

The siren call of fast food becomes deafening as you near the Marrakesh train station, flanked by familiar arches and fried-chicken acronyms – but two blocks away is this healthier, stylish, speedy lunch alternative. Daily specials typically include refreshing tomato gazpacho, mesclun greens with smoked salmon and herbed yoghurt dressing, mini quiches studded with actual ham and gooey Emmenthal cheese, and respectable coffee.

AMANDINE *Patisserie* $
☎ 0524 449612; 177 Rue Mohammed el-Beqal; ⏱ 6am-11pm; ♿

Upstanding Viennoiserie without the dreary weather and with less angsty company: Amandine is every Northern European expat's dream come true. Observe local internet daters lingering over their coffee or knocking it back

Saïda Chab
Co-owner with her sisters of Al Fassia (p48), the legendary Marrakesh restaurant started by her mother

Favourite ingredient Honestly? Onions. They're the most lowly, overlooked vegetable, but they add such richness and that velvety texture when you cook them well. **Must-have Marrakshi dishes** Try out different versions of Moroccan salads and tagines with seasonal vegetables – at the restaurant, our Berber farm tagine gets its savouriness from milk added at the last minute to wake up the spices. **Holiday treat** For Aïd al-Fitr (p164), I love *boulfef* (Moroccan tripe) – it's hard to make, but it's not a holiday without tripe, right? [laughs] **Chab family cooking secret revealed** Always buy your own ingredients from the producer; industrially raised chicken can't compare, it doesn't have the same flavour. Go straight to the source, even if it takes longer, and you'll taste the difference. My mother left home at 4.30am to get the very best vegetables for the restaurant, and for her it wasn't a hardship – it was a satisfaction.

in record time at the marble-topped espresso bar, then pop over to the sunny dessert salon for deceptively light chocolate mousse cake studded with raspberries.

🍴 AZAR *Lebanese, Moroccan $$*
☎ 0524 430920; cnr Blvd Hassan II & Rue de Yougoslavie, Guéliz; www.azarmarrakech.com; ⏲ noon-3pm &7pm-midnight; ✖ Ⓥ
Imagine a 1960s Beirut airport lounge teleported to Marrakesh via Mars, and here you have it.

As good as they look: treats at Café 16 (right)

With space-captain chairs, instant tans courtesy of orange-tinted lighting, and a DJ-remastered wall of sound gently thumping from star-patterned stucco walls, the decor is out of this world – and the Lebanese-inspired fare isn't far behind. Authenticity sticklers will appreciate the plump, tangy *shish taouk* (marinated chicken cubes), and though they may want more lemon in the hummus and more garlic in the *moutabal* (eggplant spread), a shared mezze with a Dh50 glass of respectable Moroccan wine will keep vegetarians happy and bills in this stratosphere.

🍴 BEYROUTH *Lebanese* $$
☎ 0524 423525; 9 Rue Loubnan
The best possible Lebanese response to Morocco's claim to have the supreme southern Mediterranean cuisine is the smoky, silky baba ghanoush at Beyrouth – one bite and you'll want to take some to a hammam and bathe in it. Bright, lemony, Lebanese flavours are the latest foodie trend to hit Marrakesh, and this intimate restaurant serves up the best in town at reasonable prices: a mix-and-match *mezze* (starters) for two offers enough tabbouleh, spinach pies and felafel to be a meal in itself for Dh160.

🍴 CAFÉ 16 *Patisserie* $
☎ 0524 339670; 18 Place du 16 Novembre; ⏲ 9am-midnight

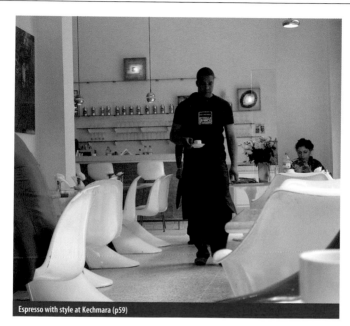
Espresso with style at Kechmara (p59)

The ultramod, citrus-and-blond-wood decor may seem oddly Dubai, but this double-height storefront of delights is an overnight sensation in the otherwise awkward, vast brick plaza of Place du Novembre 16. Coffee, tea and lunch options are respectable, but what crowds of fashionable Marrakshis queue for are fantasy versions of cake and ice cream: deliriously light multilayered raspberry mousse cake, or velvety chocolate coffee cream cake topped with gold leaf, and ice creams in such palate-waking flavours as lavender or basil and lemon.

🍴 **CATANZARO** *Italian* $$
☎ 0524 433731; 42 Rue Tariq ibn Zaid, Guéliz; ⊙ noon-2.30pm & 7.15-11pm Mon-Sat; ❌ Ⅴ
Where are we, exactly? The thin-crust, wood-fired pizza says Italy, the wooden balcony and powerful

air-con suggest the Alps, but the spicy condiments and spicier clientele are definitely midtown Marrakesh. Grilled meat dishes are juicy and generous, but the breakout star of the menu is the Neapolitan pizza loaded with capers, local olives and Atlantic anchovies.

🍽 DINO *Ice-Cream Parlour* $
☎ 0679 898703; cnr Ave Mohammed V & Rue Sebou; 🕑 7am-10pm; 🏾 👶
Beat the heat and ice-cream cravings at Dino, the most authentic gelato this side of Sicily. With a double scoop of creamy Piedmont hazelnut and dark chocolate in a gleaming, air-conditioned parlour, July in Marrakech seems perfectly reasonable – but with Sicilian blood orange and mango sorbet, it seems positively inspired.

🍽 LA TABLE DU MARCHÉ
French $$$
☎ 0524 424100; www.christophe-leroy
.com; cnr Rue Harroun Errachid & Rue des Temples
Chef Christophe Leroy remakes his St Tropez market menu Marrakesh-style, juicy and decadent: succulent filet mignon crowned with a slab of seared foie gras duck breast slathered with herbed butter, and oysters on the half-shell from nearby Oualidia – too bad the rest of the seafood menu is out of

touch with seasons and sustainability, relying on farmed salmon and monkfish. Still, the outdoor villa setting is convivial, plush seats comfy, portions large and bills gratifyingly modest.

🍽 L'ANNEXE *French* $$
☎ 0524 434010; www.lannexemarra
kech.com; 14 Rue Moulay Ali; 🕑 noon-3.30pm Sun-Fri & 7-11pm Mon-Sat; 🛜
Classic French cuisine in a mirrored cafe-bistro where you'd least expect it, on a quiet side-street in the heart of Marrakesh fashion-boutique action. A welcome switch to light, clean flavours after the umpteenth tajine: Provençale fish soup, duck confit (duck slowly cooked in its own fat) atop salad, and a mean créme brulée.

🍽 LE CHAT QUI RIT *Italian* $
☎ 0524 434311; 92 Rue de Yougoslavie;
🕑 7.30-11pm Tue-Sun; 🏾
Plenty of other places in Marrakesh serve pasta, but this place does it best: al dente, tossed with fresh produce and herbs, and drizzled with fruity olive oil. Seasonal seafood options are also a good bet, with fixings just in from the coast daily. Happy locals throng the rustic, relentlessly cheerful dining room and patio, with the namesake 'laughing cat' stencilled on sunny yellow walls, and Corsican chef-owner Bernard comes

NOUVELLE VILLE > EAT

out to ask about everyone's pasta with a gleam in his eye: he already knows the answer.

LE GRAND CAFÉ DE LA POSTE *Mediterranean* $$

☎ 0524 433038; www.grandcafedela poste.com; Blvd el-Mansour Eddahbi, cnr Ave Imam Malik; ⌚ 8am-1am

Once a French colonial hotel and favourite cafe of the dread Pasha Glaoui, this place has recently been restored to its flapper-era, potted-palm glory – minus the despots, plus two inventive chefs and the odd celebrity (hello Tom Hanks and Lawrence Fishburne). Now this landmark bistro delivers swanky comfort and a seared, herb-spiked beef tartare to write home about just behind the main post office. Prices run high for dinner, and service can be agonisingly slow – but during happy hour (6pm to 8pm), a parade of appetisers are offered with drinks, and the wine list is the best in town.

PÂTISSERIE ADAMO *Patisserie* $

☎ 0524 439419; www.traiteur-adamo .com; 44 Rue Tariq ibn Ziad; ⌚ 7am-7pm

Chocolate éclairs with élan and light custard pastries studded with berries: is that rumbling your stomach, or the sound of Parisian patisseries' thunder being stolen by this Marrakshi success? Thank

the seven saints of Marrakesh that chef Bruno Maulion saw fit to leave his Paris patisserie business, relocate to Marrakesh and raise the Marrakshi bar for croissants to the heavens.

PÂTISSERIE AL-JAWDA *Moroccan Patisserie* $

☎ 0524 433897; www.al-jawda.com; 11 Rue de la Liberté; ⌚ 8am-7.30pm; ♿ Ⓥ ♿

Care for a sweet, or perhaps 200 different ones? Hakima Alami can set you up with sweet and savoury delicacies featuring figs, orange-flower water, desert honey and other local, seasonal ingredients. Around the corner at 84 Ave Mohammed V, Hakima's savvy son has set up a tea salon featuring his mother's treats plus additional savoury items such as *briouats* (stuffed pastry 'cigars') and *khlii*, the seasoned dried Berber beef that's a very acquired taste.

PLATS HAJ BOUJEMAA *Marrakesh Specialities* $

25 Rue ibn Aicha; ⌚ noon-8pm Tue-Sun

While daredevil carnivores gnaw on dubious Djemaa grills atop rickety stools, local foodie connoisseurs calmly enjoy their scrumptious kebabs in comfy booths or the garden courtyard at Haj Boujemaa. Try to save some spicy olives and fresh bread for the parade of grilled meats, and if you're feeling adventurous, this is the place to try offal, correctly cleaned and prepared – though even when properly cooked until golden, sheep's testicles have stringy bits that stick in your teeth. That said, the chips are fantastic, and meats well-marinated.

🍴 SAMAK AL BAHRIA
Seafood $
Blvd Moulay Rachid, cnr Rue Mauritanie; 🕑 noon-10pm Tue-Sun
Another local secret hiding in plain sight, this cheerful sidewalk joint serves top-notch Moroccan-style fresh fish and chips, with perfectly tender fried calamari just in from the coast, generous chunks of lemon, and salt and cumin to season. The sign is in Arabic, but you're in the right place when there's another fish restaurant next door, a swanky cafe at the corner and a mural of happy fish unaware of their dining destiny over the counter.

🍸 DRINK
🍸 BAB HOTEL POOL LOUNGE & SKYBAB *Lounge*
☎ 0524 435250; www.babhotelmarra kech.com; Rue Mohammed el-Beqal, cnr Blvd Mohamed ed-Dahbi; 🍴 🖥 📶
Up or down? See or be the scene? Whatever your preference, you

can't go wrong at the Bab for creative cocktails in splashy settings. SkyBab offers rooftop sunsets, red carpets at your feet and the Red City cocktail: vodka, lemon and pomegranate, served up. The Pool Lounge showcases the refreshing Jack Is Back (gin, Kaffir lime, fresh ginger and fig puree), original art by emerging local artists, Marrakshi lady-DJs rocking chillout sets and Lalla Mika rainbow poufs crafted from recycled plastic bags collected from Marrakesh suburbs.

🍸 CAFÉ DES NÉGOCIANTS
Cafe
☎ 0524 435782; Place Abdel Moumen Ben Ali, cnr Ave Mohammed V & Blvd Mohammed Zerktouni; 🕑 6am-11pm; 🚼
Cafes are usually the domain of older men in Morocco, but hipsters and headscarf-clad moms mingle with the old-timers here. The regulars have seen it all before: royalty, rebel rockers, supermodels, grandmothers and after 10pm a certain type of *négociant* (businessman) in clingy Dolce & Gabbana working the Café Atlas across the street. Enjoy the show for the Dh10 price of a truly eye-opening coffee; no alcohol.

🍸 CAFÉ DU LIVRE *Cafe*
☎ 0524 432149; www.cafedulivre.com; 44 Rue Tariq ibn Ziad; 🕑 9.30am-9pm Mon-Sat

Where the literati of Marrakesh meet and flirt shamelessly over poetry discussions and wine by the glass. Join in the fray or casually eavesdrop (everyone does) as you tuck into a salad or take advantage of the wi-fi. Wall-to-wall bookshelves of new and used titles will never leave you wanting for riad reading material, and be sure to check the door downstairs for announcements of readings and other fabulous arty events.

☙ CHURCHILL BAR *Lounge*
☎ 0524 388600; www.mamounia.com; Ave Bab Jedid; ☙ 6pm-1am; ☙

Opinion remains divided over the Mamounia's estimated €120-million restoration, but critics agree: such weighty matters are best discussed over drinks at fuchsia-leather-clad, speakeasy-style Churchill Bar, named for the notable Mamounia regular. Call ahead to book, dress to impress strict doormen, and go retro with 20-year Scotch or flapper-favourite Mamoune Lady: gin, lemon and orange-flower water. At about €20 per cocktail, let heads of state buy the first round.

☙ COFFEE MARRAK'CHIC *Bar*
☎ 0644 497991; Residence al-Morad, Ave Mohammed V, Guéliz; ☙ noon-midnight; ☙

Stay cool and look cooler under canvas canopies ideal for sidewalk people-watching. Brunches here bring uptown Manhattan to downtown Marrakesh, serving champagne cocktails with bagels, bacon and pancakes – but nights here are pure Pink City, thanks to house-special Morocco Martinis (vodka, fresh mint and green tea extract), chill-out music with Berber backbeats, and flattering rosy backlighting.

☙ LE COMPTOIR *Bar*
☎ 0524 437702; www.comptoir darna.com; Rue Echouhada, Hivernage; admission free with drink or dinner; ☙ 4pm-2am; ☙

More international advances are made within the candlelit red walls of this decadent Art Deco villa than in the receiving room of the royal palace down the street. Besotted Swiss bankers lock eyes with Rabati socialites over tapas, and Italian fashionistas bat eyelashes at Moroccan musicians and French rapper MC Solar while pretending to check out the merch at the Comptoir boutique. When conversation gets too intriguing to be interrupted by squadrons of shimmying belly dancers at regular intervals, head out to the cushion-strewn courtyard. Le Comptoir is located near Hotel Imperial Borj.

NEIGHBOURHOODS

NOUVELLE VILLE

🍸 LE MELTING POT *Cafe*
☎ 0524 457773; Rue de Yougoslavie, near Tourism Office, Guéliz; ⏰ 9am-9pm; 🔣 🚻 🛜

Artists retreat within these sunburst-stuccoed walls for a welcome breather midway through Nouvelle Ville gallery crawls. Upstairs there's reliable wi-fi, sleek marble bathrooms, rotating local art shows and the inevitable chain-smoker (cough, cough); downstairs are lively art debates, sidewalk seating, and espresso strong enough to give the most staid banker action-painting impulses – or perhaps that's just a twitch? Service is attentive but not intrusive, and quite correct in boasting about their Nutella crepes.

🍸 YELLOW SUBMARINE
Lounge
☎ 0672 569864; www.yellowsub-mara kech.com; 82 Ave Hassan II, Guéliz; ⏰ 7pm-1am; 🔣

Back in Marrakesh's hippie heyday, the streets were positively littered with Rolling Stones and Beatles – and this lounge-bar intends to revive those glory days with wall-to-wall psychedelic murals, aglow with submarine-shaped lights and purple LED candles. Some anachronisms truly boggle the mind – the DJ mix of Beatles and Dire Straits, for starters, and the portrait of Al

Pacino as Scarface near the slogan 'All You Need Is Love' – but just have another Cuba Libre and go along for the ride.

⭐ PLAY
✴ ACTIONS SPORTS LOISIRS
Bicycle Hire
☎ 0661 240145; www.marrakechbike action.com; Ave Yacoub el-Mansour, Apt 4, 2nd fl, Guéliz; 2hr/half-day/full-day Dh160/260-350/620-925

Bicycles can be rented at this conveniently located spot in the centre of Nouvelle Ville – and once you've successfully navigated your first roundabout the rest of your two-wheeled adventure should be as simple as riding a bike. There are few bike lanes in Marrakesh, so requesting and wearing a helmet even in the heat is highly advisable. For a more relaxed ride without the stress of navigation, ask about guided circuits of the Palmeraie and gardens of Marrakesh (Dh260 per half-day, four-person minimum).

✴ BÔ ZIN *Club*
☎ 0524 388012; www.bo-zin.com; Douar Lahna, km3.5 Rte de l'Ourika; admission free with drink; ⏰ 8pm-1am; 🔣

Ostensibly a restaurant with Thai touches, Bô Zin's real appeal is eye candy, Asian-Moroccan architectural razzle-dazzle, and break-out performances by diners including the likes of Salma Hayek. Go late and on weekends, when it's packed; otherwise, this enormous place is a party desperately waiting to happen. It's a haul from town, so you might want to take up the offer of a chauffeur (available on request) or go with a group by taxi. It's not that far from Pacha Marrakesh (p60) if you really want to make a night/morning of it.

⭐ CANAL FORME *Gym*
☎ 0524 339580; www.marrakechcanal forme.com; 53 Ave Abou Bakker Essadik; ⏱ 8am-9pm Mon-Fri, 9am-7pm Sat, 9am-1pm Sun
Trips through the souqs are enough of a workout under normal circumstances – but when a Marrakshi invites you for a 'simple meal' at which you will inevitably be urged to eat twice your weight in roast lamb, a trip to the gym might not be such a bad idea. In addition to the gym equipment, this six-floor(!) spa and fitness centre offers squash courts, African dance classes and an indoor pool with underwater spinning classes. Prices vary depending on your choice of activity.

⭐ CINÉMA COLISÉE *Cinema*
⏱ 0524 448893; Blvd Mohammed Zerktouni, near Rue Mohammed el-Beqal;

orchestra/balcony Mon Dh20/30, Tue-Sun Dh25/35; ⏱ 3pm, 5pm, 7pm & 9.30pm
Most of the Marrakesh International Film Festival events are held at this plush cinema, so that might be David Lynch's seat you're sitting in – no wonder the evening seems a little surreal. Films are sometimes shown in the original language (English/Arabic/French), with French subtitles.

⭐ FLOWER POWER *Cafe*
☎ 0524 484087; Pépiniére Casa Botanica, Rte de Sidi Abdellah Ghiat, 3.5km past Royal Golf; www.flower-power-cafe. com; ⏱ 10am-5.30pm Wed-Sun
Getting here is a game of hide-and-go-seek: go out of town, down a driveway, through an olive grove and inside an organic plant nursery, and you'll find this organic juice bar and toddler wonderland. Squeals of delight direct you to the rabbit run, pony and donkey paddock, playhouse and play-*hanout* (grocery) where kids can pretend-haggle.

⭐ INSTITUT FRANÇAIS
Theatre, Cinema
☎ 0524 446930; www.ifm.ma; Rte de Targa, near Ave Mohammed V
Since the Théâtre Royal's indoor theatre is still under construction, this is the main year-round venue for concerts by international musicians, performances by

travelling dance troupes and independent Moroccan cinema. Flyers with program listings can be found at most Marrakshi cultural institutions, including Dar Chérifa (p98).

★ JAD MAHAL *Club*
☎ 0524 436984; 10 Rue Haroun Errachid, Hivernage; admission free with drink/dinner ; 🕑 7.30pm-2am

Through the restaurant at the far end of the courtyard, the Jad Mahal's bar is a favourite local spot to linger over cocktails by the bronze elephant until the house coverband arrives. Take the free entry to subterranean Silver, bedecked with a hundred disco balls – a subtle hint to get dancing or get out.

★ JARDIN HARTI *Park*
Rue Ouadi el-Makhazine, near Central Post Office; 🕑 8am-7pm; ♿ 🚼

Where the action is for sporty types, active kids and amateur botanists. As well as the soccer fields, there's a playground and an outdoor amphitheatre where free shows are held. The amphitheatre doubles as an after-school hangout; and there are recently restored paths through gardens of cacti and rare succulents that will test your ability to discern euphorbia from echinocactus.

★ KAWKAB JEUX
Children's Play Centre
☎ 0524 438229; www.kawkab-jeux .com; 1 Rue Imame Chafaï, near Royal Tennis Club; admission varies; 🕑 noon-10pm Tue-Fri, 10am-11pm Sat & Sun; 🚼 ♿

When your kid wearily protests at yet another carpet store, it's time for a rejuvenating visit to Kawkab Jeux. For Dh100 to Dh200 depending on the activity, you can let Junior loose on arts and crafts projects led by Kawkab's chipper staff, and buy yourself time to haggle at your leisure.

GO KAWKAB! BOO, TUNISIA!

Football fan behaviour in Morocco is generally more genteel than, ahem, England, though it always helps if you're cheering for the same team as the people sitting next to you. Usually this team is Morocco's own Lions of the Atlas, who often make it to the World Cup finals – otherwise, it's any team but Tunisia, Morocco's archrival on the field. Local teams to watch include Marrakesh's stellar Kawkab, Raja Casablanca, MAS Fez and Rabat's Fath. Support the home team and maybe your fellow fans will explain all those shouts at the referee. It's probably *'Seer al muk!'*, a shaming idiom loosely translatable as 'How can you face your mother?'.

Kids may have to be pried away from the mini-train, playground slides, video games, foosball table and snack bar.

⭐ KECHMARA *Live Music Venue*
☎ 0524 422532; 3 Rue de la Liberté, Guéliz; ◔ 8am-midnight; ⊠

Pull up a Saarinen tulip chair and stay awhile in this smartly contemporary venue with a hip Marrakshi crowd, local art, groovy music and a laid-back cocktail bar on the silvery *tadelakt* (polished plaster) terrace. Come after trawling local boutiques for a fashionably late lunch of a reasonably priced sandwich, refuel with espresso before hitting art openings up the street, and return for sunsets, the 65Dh-to-90Dh drinks and DJs or live music on the roof terrace.

⭐ LA CASA *Club*
☎ 0524 4425600; www.elandalous-marrakech.com; Hôtel el-Andalous, Ave Président Kennedy, Hivernage; admission free; ◔ 7pm-1am

The UN of world beats, where you'll witness international restaurant patrons deliver heartrending, quasi-English renditions of an Usher R&B ballad, followed by double-jointed hip shakes to Shakira and anthemic Egyptopop singalongs. Two-for-one specials on Red Bull and vodka from 7pm to 10pm get the dancing started

at the tables even before the tapas plates are cleared away, and give the neon Berber glyphs on the wall a hallucinatory glow.

⭐ LE DIAMANT NOIR *Club*
◔ 0524 446391; Hôtel Marrakech, cnr Ave Mohammed V & Rue Oum Errabia, Guéliz; admission from Dh150, including first drink; ◔ 10pm-4am; ⊠

For its rare gay-friendly clientele on weeknights and seedy charm on weekends, the gravitational pull of 'Le Dia' is undeniable. The dark dance floor thumps with hip hop and gleams with mirrors and bronzer on exposed skin, while closeted Casablanca playboys hold court at the tables and professionals lurk at the shady end of the upstairs bar. Cash only.

⭐ LE THÉÂTRO *Club*
☎ 0524 448811; www.theatromarrakech.com; Hôtel es-Saadi, Ave Qadissia, Hivernage; admission Dh250; ◔ 11pm-4.30am

Don't bother schmoozing bouncers for entry to the boring VIP area, because the dance floor is where the action is. On good nights, it's packed, sweaty, and busting dangerous moves to house, R&B and Moroc-pop; on slow nights, there's merely modest shimmying. Théâtro loves ladies: women get free shooters Mondays, free entry and drinks Tuesdays, two for one entry Wednesdays, free bubbles until 1am Thursdays, and free entry before 1am Fridays.

⭐ LES SECRETS DE MARRAKESH *Hammam*

☎ 0524 434848; 62 Rue de la Liberté, Guéliz; ⏰ 10am-8pm Mon-Sat

This ultramodern hammam in an Art Deco villa is a real find. Follow the candlelit orange niches along the graphite *tadelakt* walls to the inner sanctum, the all-black hammam. House specialities include the Atlas cedar *gommage* scrub with ginger and woodsy essential oils (Dh280), a desert sand and essential oil exfoliation (Dh 250), and the full treatment with hammam, massage, Essaouira salt scrub and the ultimate carpet-shop detox: a mint tea wrap (Dh580).

⭐ LOTUS CLUB *Club*

☎ 0524 421736; Ave Ahmed Shawki, near Rue Echouhada, Hivernage; free admission with dinner/drink; ⏰ 7.30pm-1am

Located within staggering distance of Le Comptoir and Jad Mahal disco, Lotus Club completes the supermodel night-out trifecta with bubbles, beats, and photo-ops by the white baby grand piano. Once the DJ warms up, the reverb coaxes crowds from white-padded booths onto the tiny dance floor and pool patio.

⭐ MAMOUNIA SPA & WELLNESS *Hammam*

☎ 0524 388600; Ave Bab Jedid; day pass weekday/2-day weekend Dh500/1200; 🅿 ♿ ♨

Escape city life for a day, just a 10-minute walk from Djemaa el-Fna. Mamounia's day pass lets nonguests loll in the ozone-treated pool amid songbird-filled gardens and soak in the splashy new *zellij*-paved spa (hammam, *gommage* honey scrub Dh900). With three swanky bars between the spa and the gym, you might get lost along the way. A definite value when you consider the €650 rack rate; book ahead.

⭐ PACHA MARRAKESH *Club*

☎ 0524 388405; www.pachamarrakech .com; Zone Hôteliére, Blvd Mohammed VI; admission Mon-Wed before/after 10pm free/Dh150, Thu men/women Dh150/free, Sat & Sun Dh200-300; ⏰ 8pm-1am Mon-Thu, 8pm-2am Fri-Sat; ♿

Pacha Ibiza was the prototype for this enormous disco, but Marrakesh has smashed that mould with its own international DJ line-up playing to huge weekend influxes of Casablanca hipsters and raging Rabatis. The complex includes two restaurants, Rose Bar (women drink free on Thursdays), and a pool where you can lounge in the afternoon (day entry Dh150) until the party starts – but they've got you where they want you to charge major dirhams for drinks, so savvy clubsters smuggle in water. Pacha doesn't come close to hitting its 3000 occupancy during the week, and it's a long way to come to drink alone, so bring your own entourage.

⭐ **ROYAL TENNIS CLUB**
Tennis Club
☎ 0524 431902; www.frmtennis.com; Jardin Harti, Rue Ouadi el-Makhazine; per hr Dh100; ☽ 7am-noon & 2.30-10pm
King Hassan II loved his tennis, as witnessed by numerous portraits of the guy in all-white togs at this historic 1926 tennis venue complete with clubhouse and pool. Perfect your own royal backhand with helpful instructors on one of seven clay courts (or more, depending on your aim), including the centre court named after

Moroccan tennis legend Younes el Ayanaoui. Mornings and evenings are usually best; four courts are lit at night.

⭐ **THÉÂTRE ROYAL** *Theatre*
☎ 0524 431516; 40 Blvd Mohammed VI; admission free to foyer, ticket prices vary
Tunisian architect Charles Boccara's Maghrebi monument features Egyptian Art Deco papyrus pillars, a Sahara sand-coloured portico, and showstopping Moroccan exposed brickwork in the domed foyer. Twenty-five years in the making, the Théâtre Royal is a sore subject for Marrakshis still waiting for a completed interior – apparently the work wasn't done to specifications, the money's gone, and the whole legal ordeal's become a monumental embarrassment. Meanwhile regular performances are held in a Carthage-style outdoor amphitheatre with hard seats but terrific acoustics.

> PALMERAIE

This 5260-hectare oasis 5km east of the Medina once had as many as 150,000 palm trees, but that number is dwindling fast as prime Palmeraie real estate gets snapped up for lavish hotels and private villas. To see a natural oasis, come quick – there may soon be more celebrities than trees here, unless the local nonprofit tree-planting program takes root (to help, see p157). Dromedary safaris through the palms provide prime photo ops, and cycling (bikes are available in downtown Marrakesh and from Jnane Tamsna, p133) and horseback riding are idyllic ways to take in the oasis scenery without harming its delicate ecosystem (as quads and dune buggies do). Amid the palms you might discover new talents, with cooking classes or English-language arts and crafts courses on offer. Also worth the trip from downtown Marrakesh are outstanding hammams and lounging opportunities at some of the plusher Palmeraie villa guest-houses – if you'd like to stay here, check out p133. One thing to factor into your budget is transport to/from the Palmeraie: taxis from Marrakesh will cost upwards of Dh70, and private taxi services routinely charge as much as Dh150 to Dh250 for pick-up/drop-off to Palmeraie by night.

PALMERAIE

🍽 EAT

⭐ PLAY

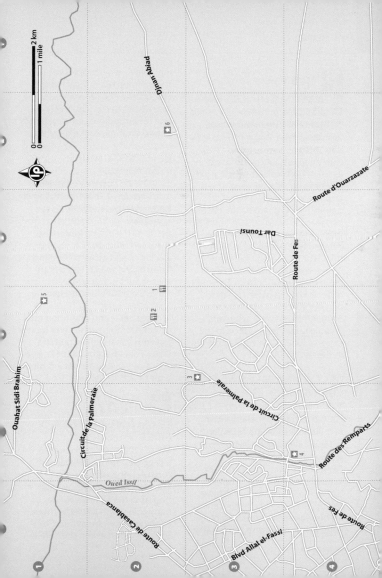

2 km
1 mile

N

Djnan Abiad

Route d'Ouarzazate

Dar Tounsi

Route de Fes

Ouahat Sidi Brahim

Circuit de la Palmeraie

Circuit de la Palmeraie

Route des Remparts

Oued Issil

Route de Casablanca

Route de Fes

Blvd Allal el-Fassi

1

2

3

4

5

6

🍴 EAT

🍴 JNANE TAMSNA COOKING CLASSES Moroccan $$$

☎ 0524 328484; www.jnanetamsna .com; Douar Abiad, Palmeraie; class incl meal Dh600; 🕐 by reservation; 🅿 🖼

Hungry for a healthy Moroccan lunch of herb-spiked salads, properly flaky bastilla, well-seasoned tagines, wine and watermelon granita? Head down to the oasis and learn to whip one up yourself under the expert tutelage of Jnane Tamsna chef Bahija, who shares her techniques and a culinary secret: aromatic produce picked mere minutes prior from Tamsna's organic kitchen gardens. Feast on your success and loll by the oxygen-filtered pool afterwards. If you'd rather leave lunch to the experts, lunch with wine and a dip in the pool is Dh400.

🍴 LE GRAND SALON AT KSAR CHAR-BAGH

Moroccan, Mediterranean $$$

☎ 0524 329244; www.ksarcharbagh. com; Djnan Abiad, off Rte de Fés; lunch incl pool & garden access Dh490; 🕐 by reservation; 🅿 🔀 🛜 🖼

Back home, you may settle for sandwiches at a desk – but at this splendid castle, lunchtime means three lavish Moroccan-Mediterranean courses and chilled wine by the reflecting pool, watch-

ing palms sway, topped with a hammam (p18). A royal feast, indeed: the chef developed signature dishes in the king's service, and his ingredients are organically grown on these castle grounds.

🍴 LES DEUX TOURS

International $$$

☎ 0524 329525; www.les-deuxtours. com; Douar Abiad, Circuit de la Palmeraie; lunch incl pool access Dh250; 🕐 by reservation; 🅿 🔀 🛜 🖼 🧍

Settle into a chaise longue by the pool or a butterfly chair on the lawn, and order something fruity from the bar: lunch is an excuse for lounging at Deux Tours. Set-price buffet lunches feature light fare – salads, sushi, dainty sandwiches – and afternoon pool access. Combine lunch and lounging with spa treatments at Les Deux Tours Hammam (p67), and you may have to be peeled off your beach towel.

⭐ PLAY

⭐ CALÈCHE-DROMEDARY RIDES

Horse Carriage, Camel Rides

pick-up/drop-off Café le Palmier d'Or, Circuit de la Palmeraie

The ultimate authenticity trip begins in the Djemaa el-Fna, bargaining with a calèche (horse carriage) driver for a round-trip to the Palmeraie and the Café le

Meryanne Loum-Martin
Parisian lawyer turned tastemaker and sustainable-travel champion as creator of Jnane Tamsna (opposite)

How Marrakesh differs from Dubai Given the great natural patrimony here, environmental impact has become an obsession. Visitors care about it too, so there's a good base for responsible tourism. **What a weekend can do** We see it all the time here: even when people come for a short break to swim or play tennis, they want to give back to the community. We encourage them to plant palms through [husband Gary Martin's] Global Diversity Foundation and support local initiatives like Dar Taliba girls' school (p157). **The well-read Red City** Café du Livre (p54) is wonderful, and at Jnane Tamsna we started a literary workshop that featured Booker Prize–winner Kirin Desai – all the proceeds went to a local literacy program. **Favourite gifts to give/get** Organic bath products from Nectarôme (see p93) and argan oil and embroidery produced by local cooperatives.

Palmier d'Or, where dromedaries snooze in the parking lot. Further negotiation will ensure your carriage awaits while you take a guided dromedary ride – Dh100 covers a 15- to 30-minute guided ride, which is usually enough time for holiday-card photo-ops.

⭐ CHEVAL PARADIS
Horseback Riding

☎ 0672 845579; www.lescavaliersde latlas.com; off Rte de Casablanca, near Palmeraie roundabout; lessons & rides from Dh350; ☺ by reservation; ♿

Dash off into the oasis on a trusty steed from this well-kept stable, which offers lessons with certified instructors, 27 well-behaved horses and sweet Welsh ponies for beginners who can't tell their bridle from their bit. Novices will appreciate classes (Dh350), which combine a half-hour of instruction with an easy 90-minute ride – or

for intermediates, a 15-minute refresher with a 2½-hour ride. Experienced equestrians up for adventure will prefer day excursions, a five-hour accompanied ride through the Palmeraie with stops for mint tea, a Moroccan lunch and snacks (Dh800).

⭐ KASBAH LE MIRAGE DROMEDARY SAFARIS
Camel Rides

☎ 0524 314444; www.kasbahlemirage .com; Ouahat Sidi Brahim

Camels seem to lurk under every palm in the Palmeraie, awaiting tourists they can lug a few blocks and then spit at, but for a longer ride on good-tempered dromedaries, Kasbah Le Mirage offers 90-minute trips (per person Dh290) – just long enough to entertain Lawrence of Arabia fantasies, but shorter than the director's cut. Just don't blame us if you discover your inner nomad

LEARN

If swaying palms leave you restless or excess lounging turns your brain to mush, consider taking a course at a Palmeraie guesthouse. Prices depend on class size and duration, and may differ for guests/nonguests. Top choices:

> Learn organic Moroccan cooking at **Jnane Tamsna** (p64; www.jnanetamsna.com) with local, sustainably sourced ingredients.

> Have the family secrets for the signature dishes of legendary restaurant Al Fassia (p48) revealed to you at cookery courses at **Bled al-Fassia** (www.bledalfassia.com).

> Make your own Moroccan-inspired crafts in English-language courses with local *maâlems* (master craftspeople) in weaving, *tadelakt* (polished plaster), *zellij* (mosaic) and *zellij* patchwork quilting at **Riad Bledna** (☎ 0661 182090; www.riadbledna.com).

Made in the shade: relax at Les Deux Tours (below)

and ditch your cushy Cairo desk job for more desert adventures.

☆ KSAR CHAR-BAGH HAMMAM *Hammam*

☎ 0524 329244; www.ksarcharbagh.com; Djnan Abiad, off Rte de Fès; P

A trip to this spectacular subterranean red-marble hammam is eerily like rebirth. Re-entry to the world is eased with scented essential oils, liberal application of Anne Semonin products and a mood-lit lounge area. There's also a swimming pool. Treat yourself to a hammam, velvety skin scrub, *rhassoul* (mud scalp rub) and 90-minute perfumed-oil massage (Dh800) and emerge vowing to be a better person – or at least wear more sunscreen.

☆ LES DEUX TOURS HAMMAM *Hammam*

☎ 0524 329525; www.les-deuxtours.com; Douar Abiad, Circuit de la Palmeraie; ☽ by reservation; P ☒

The Charles Boccara–designed domed hammam that started the mad dash on Moroccan hammams is still one of the most elegant, and now it has expanded its spa menu to lavish attention on you head to foot. The traditional hammam and *gommage* (body scrub) treatment (Dh350 to Dh450) can be upgraded with cedar-scented massage (Dh270 per 30 minutes) or soothing lavender pedicure (Dh250), a reviving dip in the pool (gratis) and upstanding cocktails (Dh70 to Dh120).

> DJEMAA EL-FNA

The magnet of Marrakesh pulls in the crowds with street theatre, magic-potion sellers, and hot rivalry at the nightly grilling competition with 100 cooks. 'La Place' sees action from dawn until well after midnight, and though you may be wary of pickpockets, makeshift food stalls and unpredictable scooter, donkey and horsedrawn-carriage traffic, don't miss the world's best dinner theatre right here. Do what you must – tuck cash into your underwear, bring your own utensils, wear reflective clothing – but by all means stick around to earn foodie bragging rights and see for yourself what new act is enthralling the crowds tonight. Just off the Djemaa are more dining adventures and the entry to the souqs; dive right in and emerge hours later overawed, bearing a carpet, and in need of an espresso at one of the Djemaa's cafes. Settle in and enjoy the show.

DJEMAA EL-FNA

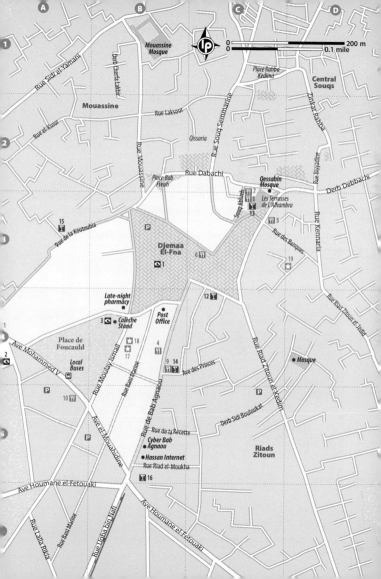

👁 SEE

👁 DJEMAA EL-FNA

🕐 **approximately 9am-1am, later during Ramadan;** ♿ 🚼

Grab a front-row or balcony seat at a cafe alongside the Djemaa, and watch the drama unfold. As the sun travels across the sky, orange-juice vendors make way for healers and henna tattoo artists, who scoot over for snake charmers, astrologers and acrobats. Around dusk, the storytellers begin their epic tales, and cooks cart in the makings of 100 restaurants specialising in barbecued everything, tasty cooked salads and steaming snails. For the ultimate dinner theatre, look no further than the Gnaoua drummers, male belly dancers and Berber musicians surrounding the Djemaa dining action. See p10 for more.

👁 KOUTOUBIA MINARET

cnr Rue el-Koutoubia & Ave Mohammed V; 🕐 **mosque & minaret closed to non-Muslims, gardens 8am-8pm**

When the present mosque and its iconic Moorish minaret were finished by Almohad Sultan Yacoub el-Mansour in the 12th century, 100 booksellers were clustered

Orange-juice vendor in Djemaa el-Fna (above)

THREE MARRAKESH MUSTS FOR DARING DINERS

> Discover a back-alley taste sensation. Adventurous eaters should try Haj Mustapha (p72), Mechoui Alley (p74) or Ben Youssef Food Stall Qissaria (p87) for truly memorable meats.
> Try argan oil at Assouss Cooperative D'Argane (p99). Chefs drizzle this oil on salads and delicate dishes for a savoury, toasted-hazelnut flavour, but you won't believe how it's made. Crafty Moroccan goats clamber up argan trees to nosh on their favourite fuzzy fruit, and then pass the pits. Traditionally women collect their dung, sort out the argan pits, split them open, and press the nuts to yield this precious oil.
> Take a Moroccan cooking class: several riads offer them to guests (p117), and La Maison Arabe (p125) offers its courses to nonguests. Jnane Tamsna (p64) teaches cooking with organic, local ingredients. Another option is **Souk Cuisine** (☎ 0673 804955; www.souk cuisine.com), where in three hours chef Gemma van de Burgt leads foodies through the Medina to pick out produce and spices and teaches them to whip up Moroccan specialities.

around its base – hence the name Koutoubia, meaning 'booksellers'. In the recently refurbished gardens outside the mosque, you might still notice a recent excavation that confirmed a longstanding Marrakshi legend: the pious Almohads were apparently distressed to discover that their lax Almoravid predecessors had built a mosque that wasn't properly aligned with Mecca, and razed the place to build another. Atop the minaret are three golden balls made of copper. The originals were reputedly real gold donated by the guilt-tripping mother of a sultan after she'd sneaked a midday snack during Ramadan. See p16 for more.

◎ RAMPARTS
calèche rides per carriage per hr Dh100
In the 12th century, the Almoravids wrapped the Medina

snugly in 19km of mud brick 5m tall, so that the city doubled as a fortress. But this didn't keep out the Almohads, who considered their predecessors irredeemably corrupt and razed the city, leaving almost no trace of their 85-year rule except for these ramparts. Today the ramparts are for lovers, not fighters, with couples patrolling the rampart gardens at sunset. Calèche (horse carriage) rides are available near the Djemaa el-Fna.

▥ EAT
▥ AL AHBAB FAST FOOD
Shwarma $
☎ 0671 377146; 70 Rue de Bab Agnaou;
⏲ 7am-11pm
The awning boasting 'recommended by Lonely Planet' must be decades old now, and still we

stand by our initial assessment of the Dh35 *shwarma* (meat sliced off a spit and stuffed into pita bread with chopped tomatoes and garnish) accompanied by four sauces and just-right French fries, with great people-watching at communal sidewalk tables. Unlike other fast-food joints along this strip, Marrakshi women frequent this place because chipper staff put everyone at ease – and the lady boss shoos away cats and troublemakers with a few choice words.

🍴 CHEZ CHEGROUNI
Moroccan à la Carte $

northeast cnr Djemaa el-Fna, near Rue des Banques; 🕐 **8am-11pm;** Ⓥ ♿
You'll need to grab a slip of paper from the plastic cup and write down your own order, but the staff could probably tell at a glance anyway: you're either a gourmand searching for the classic Dh60 tagine with chicken, preserved lemons and olives; a vegetarian in for the surprisingly flavourful, vegetable-broth-only seven-vegetable couscous; or a tagine-weary traveller in dire need of a respectable omelette with superior chips. You won't be disappointed.

🍴 DJEMAA EL-FNA FOOD STALLS *Marrakesh Specialities* $
Djemaa el-Fna; 🕐 **sunset-1am**

Around sunset, donkeys descend on the Djemaa hauling gas canisters by the cartload and all the makings of 100 small restaurants. Within the hour, the restaurants are up and running, with chefs urging passers-by to note the cleanliness of their grills, the freshness of their meat, produce and cooking oil, and their aromatic spice mixes. The grilled meats and cooked salads are cheap and often tasty, and despite alarmist warnings your stomach should be fine if you use your bread instead of rinsed utensils and stick to bottled water. Adventurous foodies will want to try Marrakesh specialities such as steaming snail soup, sheep's brain and skewered hearts – always go for the busiest stalls with the freshest meats.

🍴 HAJ MUSTAPHA
Marrakesh Specialities $

east side, Souq Ablueh (Olive Souq); 🕐 **6-10pm**
As dusk approaches, several stalls that serve *mechoui* (slow-roasted lamb) at lunchtime feature a Marrakshi speciality: paper-sealed crockpots of *tangia,* lamb traditionally slow-cooked all day in the ashes of a hammam fire. This 'bachelor's stew' is a bit messy as a takeaway order, but Haj Mustapha offers the cleanest seating despite dire bachelor decor (think

Si Ahmad Nmeis
Koutoubia Mosque muezzin, whose call to prayer is heard throughout the Mouassine from the Koutoubia Minaret (p16 and p70)

Job requirements Muezzin must give the adhan (call to prayer) on time, five times a day. Today sound systems amplify the call, but most mosques in Morocco don't use recordings. The muezzin should fill the words with their full meaning, every time. **Pure poetry** At first my job, performance was fine – I was on time, I said the words correctly, I gave the adhan facing the four cardinal directions – but I had to learn to convey the spirit of the adhan. Each word should be pronounced in such a way that it captures its poetry. **The message** The adhan begins: *Allahuakbar*, God is great. The words are simple, but each one is meaningful. All of Islam flows from that one phrase. If we can keep that in mind, we are naturally more mindful of our actions towards others. **High hopes** For people who are not Muslim and don't understand Arabic, my hope is that they sense the intention of the words, and it fills them with beauty, with comfort, with understanding.

faded photos in shattered picture frames). Use bread as your utensil to scoop up *tangia,* sprinkle it with fresh cumin and salt, and devour it with olives from the other side of the souq.

🍴 MECHOUI ALLEY
Marrakesh Specialities $

east side, Souq Ablueh; 🕑 **11am-2pm**
Around lunchtime, the vendors at this row of stalls start carving up enormous steaming sides of *mechoui,* as though King Henry VIII might show up at any moment. Step right up, point to the best-looking cut of meat and ask for a *nuss* (half) or *rubb* (quarter) kilo.

Some haggling might ensue, but Dh30 to Dh50 should procure you the freshest, most delicious falling-off-the-bone lamb you'll ever have. With your meat comes freshly baked bread, fresh cumin, salt and some olives (though you're better off picking out your own across the way). Do not attempt to sight-see or operate heavy machinery after this narcolepsy-inducing lunch – you need naps and/or four mint teas first.

🍴 PÂTISSERIE DES PRINCES
Patisserie $

☎ **0524 443033; 32 Rue de Bab Agnaou;** 🕑 **9am-9pm;** 👶 ✦

Take two ostrich eggs and call me in the morning

A sure-fire fix for blood-sugar lows, this place is beloved of kids, high-metabolism snackers and anyone stumped for something to bring to a Moroccan dinner party. The *pain au chocolat*, at Dh2.50, is a crowd-pleaser and the assorted Moroccan *petits fours* (Dh130 per kilo) are a very sweet thought indeed. There are better French pastries in the Nouvelle Ville, but for Moroccan sweets this one's hard to top.

RESTAURANT FOUCAULD
Moroccan à la Carte $

☎ 0524 440806; Ave el-Mouahidine, cnr Place de la Foucauld; ⏲ noon-3pm & 7.30pm-midnight; Ⓥ

This stucco-bedecked, dimly lit restaurant has seen many a Moroccan wedding in its day – which was at least 30 years ago, judging from copper relief landscapes from the 1970s and Bureau of Tourism posters from the French Protectorate. But this place is definitely set for a comeback with succulent lamb with figs and sesame, fresh crusty bread, and tangy *harira* (soup), all for Dh100.

VENEZIA ICE
Ice-Cream Parlour

www.venezia-ice.com; 279 Ave Mohammed V; ⏲ 9am-10pm; ♿ ♿

Heavenly treats for hot days, right across the street from the Koutoubia: rich ice creams and tangy sorbets, made by a Casablanca-based company and scooped to order. While the gelato's not strictly Venetian, it comes in worldly flavours, like mango, *frutti di bosco* (wild berry) and green tea, that would do Marco Polo proud. Free tastes make tough choices easier.

🍸 DRINK

🍸 CAFÉ DU GRAND BALCON
Cafe

south side, Djemaa el-Fna, near Rue Riad Zitoun el-Kedim; ⏲ 8am-10pm; ♿

The best spot to catch all the action in the Djemaa, with permanent crowds on the front patio to prove it. Older gents hang out inside to avoid the jostling and panhandling on the patio, but only families and clandestine lovers actually go upstairs to the quiet 'grand balcon', where service is erratic at best. The OJ here is not freshly squeezed, but there are mean espressos, frothy cappuccinos, and proper tea with mint or steamed milk. Technically this place serves ice cream, but there's better around the corner at Venezia Ice (p75).

☷ LES TERRASSES DE L'ALHAMBRA *Cafe-Bar*

☎ 0524 427570; northeast cnr, Djemaa el-Fna; ☷ 8am-midnight; ☷ ☷ V

By day, the tasteful Moroccan-modern decor is a sight for souq-sore eyes, and Italian Illy espresso served under terrace tent awnings will sharpen your wits for bargaining. Diners get dibs on the cushy first-floor seats on the first floor, but you're better off sticking with tangy lemon tarts on the upper terraces. The somewhat slow, snippy service is understandable given all those steep stairs, and besides, what's the hurry? Stick around to watch potion-sellers whip up good-luck charms and storytellers draw the crowds at sunset.

☷ MARRA-BOOK CAFÉ *Cafe*

☎ 0524 376448; http://marrabook. e-monsite.com; 53 Derb Kabada, off Ave des Princes; ☷ 10am-10pm

The plot twists as you turn off action-packed Rue de Bab Agnaou into a dubious-looking *derb* (winding alley), only to discover this mellow three-storey literary cafe. The ground-floor bookstore sells a range of paperbacks in French and English, from novels to cookbooks and keepsake architecture books. Upstairs, coffee and tea are served in the salon amid rotating photo exhibitions, and visitors turn book

pages between thoughtful pulls on water-pipes. Basic tagines, goat's-cheese salad and 'Berber burgers' are served on low tables on the breezy, cushion-strewn terrace, where conversation flows easily and sunny days become starlit nights.

☷ PIANO BAR LES JARDINS DE LA KOUTOUBIA *Bar*

☎ 0524 388800; www.lesjardinsdelakou toubia.com; Les Jardins de la Koutoubia Hotel, 26 Rue el-Koutoubia; ☷ 5pm-1am

How often has the long-suffering pianist heard 'Play it again, Sam'? Probably too many to count, but he'll gamely play 'As Time Goes By', because it's that sort of classy joint. Like the fabulous hotel lobby, the decor here is all restrained Moroccan modernity, from its natural cedar ceilings to the plush Berber carpets – a fine place to unwind after your tour of duty in the souqs. Alcohol is served.

☷ RESTAURANT/BAR DU GRAND HOTEL TAZI *Bar*

☎ 0524 442787; Ave el-Mouahidine, cnr Rue de Bab Agnaou; ☷ 7pm-1am

For those who object to a Dh40 bottle of beer as a matter of prole-tarian principle, this place serves the cheapest in town at Dh25 to throngs of like-minded travellers and Marrakshis just off work in the souqs. The tales take a turn for the outrageous as the evening wears on, but then some of us enjoy that kind of thing.

⭐ PLAY

⭐ CINÉMA EDEN *Cinema*
Derb Dabbachi, near Rue des Banques; tickets Dh15; 🕑 **shows at 3pm, 6pm & 9pm**
You don't know how rowdy cinema can get until you've caught a romantic comedy with the usually all-male audience in this mudbrick movie house tiled with broken plates, plastered with Bollywood posters and carpeted with peanuts. As Juan Goytisolo explains in *Cinema Eden: Essays from the Muslim Mediterranean*, only films with happy endings are allowed here – the management prefers evenings here to be a laugh riot, rather than any other kind.

⭐ HOTEL ALI BIKE RENTAL *Bicycle Hire*
☎ **0524 444979; Rue Moulay Ismail**
No frills here, and no 20-speed mountain bikes either – but if the warhorse on offer still looks good after you kick the tyres and test the brakes, you'll have a whole new way to get around the Medina. As for dealing with Marrakshi traffic: ask about helmets, and consider prayer.

⭐ MEDINA SPA *Hammam*
☎ **0524 385059; www.medina-spa -marrakech.com; 27 Derb Zaari, off Rue des Banques;** 🕑 **9.30am-9pm**
Steps from the dusty Djemaa, enjoy a deep steam-clean, brisk scrub and rejuvenating massage at the right price (30-minute hammam & *gommage* Dh100, massage Dh330 per hour). Saunas and massage rooms are private, and couples or friends can get spa treatments together. This is a busy riad-spa, so expect a certain amount of noise, line-dry-damp (though clean) robes, and foot traffic on the steep, narrow stairs (watch your footing in those borrowed plastic slippers). Walk-ins are welcome, but expect a wait.

> CENTRAL SOUQS & DERB DEBACHI

Souq means 'market', but when locals refer to 'the souqs' they mean the maze of market streets north of the Djemaa el-Fna and southwest of the Musée de Marrakesh. The main thoroughfare from the Djemaa el-Fna, Souq Semmarine (Leather Souq), sells a hodgepodge of local crafts, but further north the souqs are more specialised. Wander the east–west *qissarias* (covered markets) between Souqs Smata and el-Kebir (literally, 'the big souq for leatherwork') and buy direct from leather toolers, basket weavers, woodworkers and felt makers. There's another *qissaria* to the west of Koubba Ba'adiyn packed with food stalls where you can join the locals for lunch. And you'll soon discover that specialist souqs with the same names can be found elsewhere, just when you thought you knew where you were.

CENTRAL SOUQS & DERB DEBACHI

◉ SEE

Ali ben Youssef Medersa	1	B2
Criée Berbère (Carpet Souq)	2	B4
Dar Bellarj	3	B2
Jewellers Souq	4	A3
Koubba Ba'adiyn	5	B2
Maison de la Photographie	6	C2
Musée de Marrakech	7	B2
Rahba Kedima	8	B4
Souq Sebbaghine (Dyers Souq)	9	A3
Souq Smata (Slipper Souq)	10	A3
Souq Ableuh (Olive Souq)	11	A5
Souq Cherratine (Leather Souq)	12	B3
Souq Haddadine (Metalworkers' Souq)	13	A3
Souq Kchacha (Fruit & Nut Souq)	14	A5
Souq Kimakhine (Musical Instrument Makers Souq)	15	A3
Souq Lebbadine	16	B2
Souq Sebbaghine	17	C3
Souq Semmarine (Leatherworkers Souq)	18	B3

🛍 SHOP

Abdelatif Instruments	19	A3
Abedelatif El Maanaoui	20	A3
Bob Music	21	B5
Cooperative Artisanale Femmes de Marrakech	22	A3
Faissal Bannouna	23	C2
Michi	24	B3
Mohammed Ben el-Hair	25	B3
Moulay Youssef el Alaoui	26	A3
Sadek	27	A4
Sidi Ahmad Gabaz Stucco	28	B3
Zenobie	29	A3

🍴 EAT

Ben Youssef Food Stall Qissaria	30	A2
Dar TimTam	31	B4
Le Foundouk	32	C2
Souk Kafé	33	A2

🍷 DRINK

Café des Épices	34	A4

⭐ PLAY

Bain d'Or	35	B2

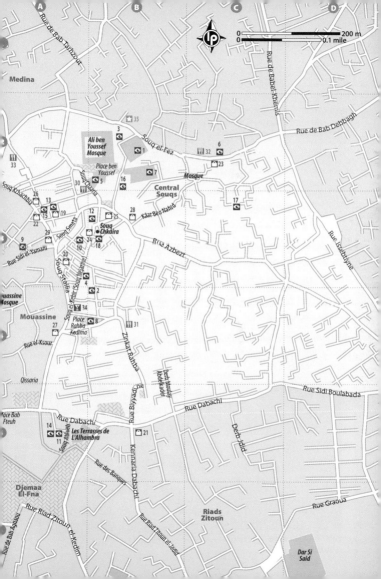

NEIGHBOURHOODS

CENTRAL SOUQS & DERB DEBACHI

There are a few cafes at the northeast end of the souqs where you can grab a bite and catch your breath, but the action-packed central souqs are not the best place to unwind. To really experience the raucous/peaceful contrast that is the essence of Marrakesh, adjacent Derb Debachi is a calming residential area with stunning riads (see p127), and you'll find more historic riads in the Mouassine.

SEE

ALI BEN YOUSSEF MEDERSA
☎ 0524 441893; Place Ben Youssef; admission Dh50, with Musée de Marrakesh & Koubba Ba'adiyn Dh60; 🕑 9am-6pm; 👶 ✗

This centre of Quranic learning was founded in the 14th century, and in its heyday 900 students spent all day, every day, studying religious and legal texts. A couple of the 2nd-floor 3-sq-metre dorm rooms on the west side of the courtyard show how students lived – but they must've been a seniors' rooms, because there are many smaller ones in courtyards down the hall with sleeping lofts up makeshift ladders for a truly monastic existence. The school was updated in the 19th century, but the limited bathrooms proved a persistent problem. The medersa still exudes magnificent, studious calm – and now that tourists have the run of the place, the bathrooms are top notch. See p14 for more.

DAR BELLARJ
☎ 0524 444555; Ali ben Youssef Medersa; admission free except some events; 🕑 9.30am-12.30pm & 2-5.30pm Mon-Sat during exhibitions; 👶

Flights of fancy come with the territory at Dar Bellarj, a stork

Just drink it – beautiful skin guaranteed

THE SOUQ CIRCUIT

Put your sense of direction to the ultimate test with this loop of the central souqs:

> Souq Ableuh: make like James Bond and follow the scent of 1000 martinis to the Olive Souq.
> Souq Kchacha: find your dream date in stall after stall of dried fruits in the Fruit and Nut Souq.
> Souq Semmarine: trendy handbags and handy manbags lure luggage fetishists in the Leather Souq.
> Criée Berbère (Souq Joutia Zrabi): the namesake 'Berber Call' can be heard Saturday to Tuesday around 4pm, when Atlas Mountain dealers descend for auctions in the covered Carpet Souq – but you'll be called into shops 'just for looking' anytime.
> Souq Cherratine: for centuries, equestrians have exhibited unbridled passion for the hand-tooled saddles in the Leatherworkers' Souq.
> High-Tech Souq: donkey carts haul in flat-screen TVs and computers in this anachronistic mudbrick multimedia marketplace.
> Souq Haddadine: sparks fly and hammers clang in the Blacksmiths' Souq, where old bikes become the latest lanterns; forge on to…
> Souq Kimakhine: musicians dawdle for days watching lutes carved and tambourines stretched in the Instrument-Makers' Souq; buy a drum and beat it to…
> Souq Sebbaghine: you've saved the most spectacular souq for last – the Dyers' Souq has yarn hanging from the rafters in primary colours. Wander past the bubbling vats of dye and if you're in the right Souq Sebbaghine you can head down Rue el-Mouassine back toward the Djemaa. Then it becomes official: you're a dyed-in-the-wool souq specialist.

See p12 for more.

hospital (*bellarj* is Arabic for stork) turned into Marrakesh's nonprofit arts centre. Each year Dar Bellarj adopts a program theme, recently including storytelling through film and women's textiles. Arabic calligraphy demonstrations, art openings, crafts exhibits and arts workshops are regular draws for locals and visitors alike, and a 20Dh coffee in the salon full of art books makes a blissful break from the souqs.

☐ KOUBBA BA'ADIYN

opposite Ali ben Youssef Mosque; admission with Musée de Marrakesh & Ali ben Youssef Medersa Dh60; 🕙 **9am-6pm**
The Almohads sought to erase all trace of their predecessors, but they mysteriously spared this small, graceful 12th-century cupola for ablutions. This is your crib sheet for Hispano-Moresque architecture, with keyhole arches, a well-proportioned dome on a crenulated base, and interlaced carved arabesques.

☉ MAISON DE LA PHOTOGRAPHIE

☎ 0524 385721; www.maison-dela photographie.com, in French; 46 Rue Fassi; admission adult/child Dh40/free; ◷ 9.30am-7pm; ♿

Art collectors Patrick Menac'h and Marrakshi Hamid Mergani opened this riad gallery to show-case vintage Moroccan photog-raphy in its original context. Fascinating, well-documented works from 1870 ro 1960 include a 1907 Djemaa el-Fna vista, a 1920 photo of Ali ben Youssef Medersa with students, and a rare, full-colour 1957 docu-mentary shot in Morocco. Don't miss the panoramic terrace for eye-opening coffee and fragrant chicken tagine at a starving-artist price (35Dh).

☉ MUSÉE DE MARRAKESH

☎ 0524 390911; www.musee demarrak ech.ma, in French; Place ben Youssef; admission Dh40, with Koubba Ba'adiyn & Ali ben Youssef Medersa Dh60; ◷ 9am-6.30pm; ♿

Once you've settled into a sofa in its *zellij*-bedecked *bhous* (seat-ing nooks), mesmerised by the golden light of the courtyard and its burbling fountains, you might want to stay awhile – or forever. But it wasn't always so peaceful at

ESSENTIAL BARGAINING BANTER

A little friendly banter brings better prices and good feelings all around. Here's what you need to know to bargain like a local:

asmeetek?	What's your name?
metsherrfin	Honoured to meet you.
kulshi bikher?	Everything's good?
lubes, burakallahuafik/i	Fine, bless you.
saha labes?	Your health is good?
laliha labes?	Your family's good?
allah yrhem waldik/i ...	If it's no trouble ... (when asking or receiving help; lit. 'May God protect your parents')
wakha nshufha?	May I look at it?
makein mushkil	No problem.
bshhal?	How much is it?
akhir taman shhal?	What's the last price?
zhmaha li afak	Please wrap it.
allahyakhlef	May it be returned to you. (when receiving money or hospitality)
ma'asalama, sahbee	With peace, my friend.

this palace. Original owner Mehdi Mnebhi had a spectacular rise and fall as the minister of defence under Sultan Moulay Abdelaziz, who was first decorated by Queen Victoria then betrayed by England and forced to flee to Tangiers. Like most other nice digs in Marrakesh at the time, the palace was snatched up by colonial conspirator Pasha Glaoui. After independence it briefly became a girls' school, but it has since been restored by the Omar Benjelloun Foundation as a showplace for Moroccan traditional arts and travelling art shows. Outside, there's a courtyard cafe serving powerful espresso, and a bookshop with a limited selection of art books. See p22 for more.

🄲 RAHBA KEDIMA

off Souq Nejarine; ⏲ 9am-8pm
Harry and the Hogwarts crowd probably shop here for school supplies. The Rahba Kedima is ringed with apothecaries who sell exotic and mysterious spell supplies to locals and traditional cosmetics to tourists, who eagerly dip a wet finger into clay pots of *aker* and smear it on their lips as rouge – apparently unaware that this stuff is made of ground-up insects.

🛍 SHOP

⬚ ABDELATIF INSTRUMENTS
Musical Instruments
86 Souq Kchachbia, near Souq Haddadine; ⏲ 9.30am-6pm
Musicians make pilgrimages to the lute-maker's souq to watch beautiful music in the making, and here you can glimpse *maâlem* (master craftsman) Sidi Abdelatif carving lutes, tambourines, *ginbris* (two-stringed banjos) and *ribabs* (single-stringed fiddles). Since you're buying straight from the artisan himself, you can customise yours and get a better deal, too – music to every starving musician's ears.

⬚ ABEDELLATIF EL MAANAOUI
Moroccan Crafts, Fashion
☎ 0667 763728; Souq Kharrazine el-Bali, off Souq Semmarine; ⏲ 10am-7pm Sat-Thu
Distinctive, worldly garments with luxe textures to make any occasion: plush plum velvet jackets deserve US concert tours, navy cotton sateen women's shifts merit invites to English royal weddings, and traditional ivory wool *trâa* (free-form tunics) make entrances at Berlin art gallery openings. Nubby, handwoven wool in natural shades of brown and grey makes excellent blankets or made-to-order coats.

⚐ BOB MUSIC
Musical Instruments

☎ 0666 745200; Rue Dabachi

In case you hadn't noticed the Bob Marley posters and music in shops throughout the souqs, this store makes the Marrakesh-Jamaica connection even more obvious. Gnaoua musicians are quick to point out the similarity in some rhythmic patterns and tunes, but you can put this ethnomusicology theory to the test yourself: pick up some Gnaoua castanets or a drum in this shop, and try your own Gnaoua rendition of 'Redemption Song'. No matter how badly you play it, you're bound to make their day at Bob Music.

⚐ COOPERATIVE ARTISANALE FEMMES DE MARRAKECH
Moroccan Crafts

☎ 0524 378308; 67 Souq Kchachbia;
🕙 10am-1pm & 3.30-7pm Sat-Thu

Fair trade never looked so stylish. When Souad (opposite) and nine Marrakshi women artisans wound up with overstock and design ideas from a big American order for snappy, linen-cotton blend tunics, they realised they could skip the middleman and sell their own modern designs right in Marrakesh. With a small grant, they've set up this boutique and made connections with other cooperatives whose work they sell

at low, fixed prices in a small annex. Products include sustainably harvested thuya wood bowls from Essaouira, Safi tea sets and small Middle Atlas rugs.

⚐ FAISSAL BANNOUNA
Moroccan Crafts, Fashion

☎ 0664 081287; Rue Fassi; 🕙 10am-6.30pm Sat-Thu

Young *mâelem* (master craftsman) Faissal is a third-generation weaver bringing fashion-forward style to the family tradition. From gossamer filaments of polished cotton and linen, he hand-weaves wave-patterned hammam wraps in sea-foam blue and table runners the colour of sunsets on Marrakesh ramparts. Fixed prices.

⚐ MICHI *Fashion, Housewares*

☎ 0661 864407; http://michi-morocco.com, in Japanese; 21 Souq Kchachbia;
🕙 10am-7pm Mon-Thu & Sat

When an intrepid Japanese traveller met a hip Marrakshi designer, they discovered a shared love for craft, reclaimed materials and *wabi-sabi* (organic forms). Hicham and Michiko now have a family and this highly original boutique, featuring designs made with reclaimed materials, spare forms and a whimsical sense of humour: *babouches* (slippers) made from flour sacks, mirrors made of salvaged Libya oil drums,

Souad Boudeiry
Medina fashionista and fair trade trendsetter for Cooperative Artisanale Femmes de Marrakech (opposite)

Favourite places in the Medina Besides my neighbourhood? The Djemaa el-Fna is its own city, and you can take it all in from Café du Grand Balcon (p75) – it's always fascinating, no matter how many times you see it. The souqs are a theatre, and every day is a new act. From one word, these guys can make a joke! **Marrakshiyya fashion statements** The modern kaftan has smart details: colour contrasts, or no sleeves, or a distinctive neckline. I don't wear *djellabas* [robes] often, but a well-tailored one makes great evening wear. **The look for men** Traditionally, it's an embroidered *trâa* [large, square tunic with slit arm-holes] and bright yellow *smata* [slippers] – but now maybe with jeans. **Marrakshiyyas on the move** The women's revolution is already here: we're in every profession, we're in Parliament, we're not hiding. We have the same problems as any other working women, but we know our rights and we're claiming them.

and hammam totebags made with recycled feed bags. Prices are fixed; you won't find these original designs elsewhere.

🛍 MOHAMMED BEN EL-HAIR
Carpets
284 Draze Souq el-Kebir, near Musée de Marrakesh; ⏰ **9am-7pm**
Mt Everest is overrated; the most thrilling mountain to scale is the one of colourful Berber carpets in this tiny shop. Charming elderly proprietor Abu Mohammed ushers you in with a smile and mint tea, then waves towards the mountain with a single word: 'Democracy!' This is your invitation to clamber up, and pull down whatever carpets appeal to you. The prices are more than democratic; they're downright proletarian.

🛍 MOULAY YOUSSEF EL ALAOUI
Moroccan Crafts, Housewares
☎ 0524 440498; www.creation-passi menterie.com; 2 Souq el-Kimakhine; ⏰ 10am-6.30pm Mon-Thu & Sat-Sun
For small gifts, this place has all the trimmings. *Passimenterie* is the art of trim, including tassels, braiding and ingenious knotting, and here the Moroccan tradition is turned into multistrand silk necklaces, knotted key rings, clever braided bookmarks and grand curtain ties finished with 60cm-long suede tassels. From

the doorway, this looks like just another tunic shop, but those in the know head right upstairs to the accessories section. Fixed prices.

🛍 SADEK
Moroccan Crafts, Housewares
☎ 0613 718583; 63 Souq Nejarine; ⏰ 10am-7pm Sat-Thu, 10am-1pm Fri
Flowers blooming mean spring has arrived – or you've arrived at Sadek, where pillows, bedspreads and poufs (ottomans) are covered with embroidered wildflowers. The graphic, spiky flowers are traditionally from Rabat, but applied to sleek housewares in silver, orange, or lilac, they're pure Marrakesh.

🛍 SIDI AHMAD GABAZ STUCCO *Moroccan Crafts*
2 Souq Shaaria; ⏰ 9.30am-6pm Sat-Thu, 9am-noon Fri
Like any visitor with 20/20 vision, you may already be awestruck by the stucco detail up the street at the Ali ben Youssef Medersa – and this is your chance to take home a piece of the stucco action. Sidi Ahmad carves traditional geometric and floral designs right in his shop as well as sweet nothings in French, but with a day's turnaround he will very graciously carve your house number or whatever you like in English…just don't get any four-letter ideas, you naughty people.

🏠 ZENOBIE *Moroccan Crafts, Housewares*

☎ 0666 078087; 7 Souq Kchachbia; 🕐 10am-7pm Mon-Thu & Sat

A Parisian–Moroccan couple are the inspired design team behind this new global-chic boutique, showcasing one-of-a-kind household and fashion accessories with handmade Moroccan flair. Indian silk scarves are minutely embroidered with Moroccan mosaic patterns; terracotta dishes are painted with henna wedding designs; Limoges teapots get reconstructed and reinforced with Marrakshi hammered silver; and twisting gazelle's horns serve as handles on Italian coffee pots. Prices are fixed and not inexpensive, but don't think it over too long – limited stock changes daily with the designers' latest inspiration.

🍴 EAT

🍴 BEN YOUSSEF FOOD STALL QISSARIA

Marrakesh Specialities $

off Souq Shaaria, near Koubba Ba'adiyn; 🕐 11.30am-3.30pm

Just around the corner from the Koubba Ba'adiyn is a labyrinth of *qissarias* lined with stalls serving tagines, steaming snails, and the occasional stewed sheep's head hot off the Libya gas burner. Tourists at food stalls in the Djemaa el-Fna may think they're being adventurous, but the *qissarias* are where the real action is. Eat whatever looks fresh and tasty, even if you have to wait for a free stool.

🍴 DAR TIMTAM

Moroccan à la Carte $

☎ 0524 391446; Zinkat Rahba, near Rahba Kedima; 🕐 11.30am-4pm; **V** 🚻

Head through the rug shop and hang a right into this 18th-century riad's innermost courtyard, where you'll find cushioned nooks and an à la carte menu (you may have to request it). Some menu items are overpriced (the Dh200 tangia, for example), but a rejuvenating mint tea and a generous assortment of eight Moroccan salads (Dh95)

Setting the mood at Le Foundouk (p88)

NEIGHBOURHOODS

CENTRAL SOUQS & DERB DEBACHI

makes a fine light lunch amid the songbirds.

🍴 LE FOUNDOUK

Moroccan Fusion $$

☎ 0524 378190; www.foundouk.com; 55 Souq el-Fez, near Ali ben Youssef Medersa; 🕑 noon-1am

Push past the studded doors and you've entered a movie where the lighting is perfect, the sets are breathtaking and everyone is good-looking. This 18th-century riad sets the scene in shades of ivory, black and deep purple, crowned with a spidery iron chandelier straight out of a Tim Burton movie. Silk-costumed waiters glide from one private seating nook to the next like butterflies, bearing fresh strawberry juice, Casa beer and champagne Bellinis with fresh peach juice. Square henna lamps with fringes made from cloves set the mood for a savoury *bastilla* (pigeon pie), which is so much easier to appreciate when it's not the third of five courses. Don't miss a trip to the terrace for your establishing shot of Marrakesh.

🍴 SOUK KAFÉ *Morrocan* $

☎ 0662 610229; 11 Derb Souk Jedid, near Rue Riad Laarouss; 🕑 9am-9pm; 🔀 Ⓥ

One fresh OJ coming up, at Café des Épices (opposite)

Pull up a hand-hewn stool under terrace sun umbrellas and stay awhile: this is authentic local food to savour. The Moroccan *meze* of six savoury cooked vegetable dishes qualifies as lunch for two, and the vegetarian Berber cous-cous is surprisingly hearty – but wait until you get a whiff of their aromatic Marrakshi *tangia*, beef that flakes apart after its morning slow-cooking in a hammam just across the street (one feeds two people).

DRINK

CAFÉ DES ÉPICES *Cafe*
☎ 0524 391770; Rahba Kedima; ⏱ 8am-9pm

Grab a prime spot above the healers and potion-dealers of the Rahba Kedima and watch the magic happen as you sip a reviving caffeinated beverage. The young Marrakshi staff are hip and easygoing, there's free wi-fi, and if you linger over mint tea long enough, the rooftop terrace offers a sunset view of the souqs. Salads and sandwiches are made to order – try the chicken spiked with herbs, nutmeg and olives.

 PLAY

BAIN D'OR *Hammam*
Derb Zaouiat Lakhdar, near Ali ben Youssef Medersa; men Dh8, women Dh10, gommage extra; ⏱ men 6-11am & 8.30pm-midnight, women 11am-8.30pm

This is your friendly neighbour-hood public hammam, small and lovely with stuccoed detail and sunlight filtering through the dome. As at all public hammams, bring your own plastic mat, flip-flops, towel and a change of undies – you'll be expected to wear yours.

> BAB DOUKKALA & DAR EL-BACHA

Just out of earshot of Djemaa el-Fna crowds and the hustle of the souqs, this neighbourhood is a prime place to see what the Medina is like in its downtime. Women linger to chat outside community hammams, kids pull on parents' hands as they pass carts loaded with sesame sweets, and students throng cybercafes to make kissy faces at their latest love interests via webcam. Take a cue from the locals and relax, already: right behind the major routes and food souqs you'll find tranquil riads and fabulous restaurants, and a short walk away are the clubs and restaurants of Nouvelle Ville. Through Bab Doukkala (Doukkala Gate) is the busy CTM bus station, and coming back from clubs late at night you'll want to know where you're going to avoid minor hassle. But generally the neighbourhood looks after its own, and within a day or two of staying here and saying hello to the lady who feeds local cats on her front stoop, that includes you.

BAB DOUKKALA & DAR EL-BACHA

🛍 SHOP
Bab Doukkala
Food Souq 1 B2
Boutique Noir d'Ivoire ...2 C1
Mohammed Rida
Ben Zouine 3 D3
Mustapha Blaoui 4 D3
Pharmacie Koutoubia 5 D5

🍴 EAT
Dar Moha 6 D3
La Maison Arabe
Restaurant 7 C4
Marrakesh Korner 8 D3
Riad 72 ....9 D3

📺 DRINK
La Maison Arabe Bar ...(see 7)

⭐ PLAY
Hammam Bab Doukkala 10 C3
Hammam Dar el-Bacha 11 D5
Maison Arabe ....(see 7)

A

- Gare Routière

B

- To Bab el-Khemis (1.2km)

C

- Rue el-Gaza
- 2

D

- P

N 0 ——————— 100 m
0 ——————— 0.05 miles

Bab Doukkala
P

rue Bab Doukkala

rue Mohammed el Mefkakh

rue Boutouil

Bab Doukkala

1

To Librairie Dar el-Bacha (50m)

4   3
8
rue Bab Doukkala
10

6

Bab Doukkala Mosque

Derb Zaouia

Arest Awzel

9

7   Derb Assebbe

rue Fatima Zohra

rue Dar el-Glaoui

Mouassine

rue Iben Lakhdar

11

Town Hall

rue Fatima Zohra

5

rue Sidi el-Yamani

CyberPark

Municipal Pool

rue Abbes Sebti

Ave Mohammed V

SHOP

BAB EL-KHEMIS MARKET
Market

**Bab el-Khemis, Medina ramparts;
⏱ 8am-3pm Thu & Sun**

Ever wondered where riads get all those sand-worn carved wooden doors, Art Deco stained-glass windows, Mamounia-engraved silver spoons and porcelain inkwells? Follow the stampede of riad owners Thursday and Sunday mornings to outside Bab el-Khemis (Thursday Gate), where sharp eyes and even sharper bargaining skills could help you score one-of-a-kind treasures.

BAB DOUKKALA FOOD SOUQ *Food*

**Rue Fatima Zohra, btwn Bab Doukkala Mosque & Bab Doukkala bus station;
⏱ 9am-8pm**

Less touristy than the central souqs and easier to navigate, this neighbourhood market is a prime spot to pick up spices, preserved lemons, earthenware tagines and other gourmet goodies, plus fresh fruit and baked goods.

BOUTIQUE NOIR D'IVOIRE
Fashion, Beauty Products

☎ 0524 380975; www.noir-d-ivoire .com; Riad Noir d'Ivoire, 31 Derb Jedid Bab Doukkala; ⏱ usually noon-6pm & by appointment

Sure, you could spend days digging in the souqs for elusive

treasures, wired on mint tea – or you could just head directly to this boutique, where style trendsetter Jill Fechtman has thoughtfully done all the footwork for you. Find sought-after botanical Sens de Marrakesh products, as well as custom cloaks and eveningwear by Mohammed Rida ben Zouine in the riad's trademark black and ivory. You can even enjoy a cocktail in the courtyard afterward.

LIBRAIRIE DAR EL-BACHA
Bookshop

☎ 0524 391973; 14 Rue Dar el-Bacha; ⏱ 9am-1pm & 3-7.30pm

A fine selection of cookbooks, art books, and postcards, plus stamps to send them and some wonderful antique Moroccan stamps to take to all your philatelist friends back home. Bookshop owner Noureddine Tilsaghani is also a photographer, and you can pick up some of his atmospheric shots of Marrakesh here. There's a fantastic selection of Moroccan literature and poetry in (mostly French) translation.

MOHAMMED RIDA BEN ZOUINE *Fashion*

☎ 0524 385056; 142 Rte Arset Aouzal; ⏱ 10am-7pm Sat-Thu

Saville Row tailors would bite their thimbled thumbs with envy at Ben Zouine's custom hand-finished men's shirts, curve-skimming linen dresses with handmade silk closures and snappy hooded jackets in 'Moroccan cashmere' (thick combed-cotton flannel). Sidi Mohammed keeps tabs on the latest men's suit styles from Belgium, and can make you a slimming, bitter chocolate brown suit with a sneaky orange lining that Dries van Noten might admire.

MUSTAPHA BLAOUI
Housewares
☎ 0524 385240; 142-4 Rue Bab Doukkala; 9am-8pm

The next best thing to taking your riad home would be to take home all those fabulous furnishings – and with Mustapha Blaoui's generous shipping policy and stock of everything from hand-embroidered coverlets to inlaid rolltop desks, that's actually possible. Some items are imported from India, so if you want to bring home a Marrakshi speciality, just ask the easygoing staff to point you toward the locally produced goods.

PHARMACIE KOUTOUBIA
Pharmacy & Beauty Products
☎ 0524 381072; Ave Fatima Zohra, cnr Rue Sidi el-Yamani

All the essentials you forgot to bring are here, plus fragrant

In stitches: Mohammed Rida Ben Zouine (opposite)

Nectarôme skin- and hair-care products from the organic gardens in nearby Ourika Valley. If you're not feeling your best, just tell the sharp young pharmacist what's wrong – she'll point out the best pharmaceutical or homeopathic cures for what ails you.

EAT
DAR MOHA
Moroccan Fusion $$$
☎ 0524 386400; www.darmoha.ma; 81 Rue Dar el-Bacha; 12-3pm & 7.30pm-midnight Tue-Sun; V

Chef Mohammed Fedal is Morocco's foremost celebrity chef, and at his flagship restaurant you can tell why. The Marrakshi maverick tickles tastebuds with witty, imaginative takes on Moroccan classics: quail in a flaky *warqa* (pastry) nest, foie gras and argan oil couscous, melon 'couscous' with thyme honey. Lately you're as likely to catch Chef Moha on YouTube as in the kitchen – but lunch by the pool is a reliable feast, with orange-flower scented cucumbers and spice-rubbed lamb chops (Dh220; wine extra).

🍽 LA MAISON ARABE RESTAURANT *Moroccan* $$$
☎ 0524 387010; www.lamaisonarabe.com; 1 Derb Assehbe; ⏲ 7.30pm-midnight; ✂ V
La Maison Arabe was serving Moroccan fine dining decades before other riads, and viva la *diffa* (feast) difference: here the focus is on the food and company, get-cozy booth seating, excellent classical Andalusian musicians instead of cheesy belly dancers, and the humble Marrakshi *tangia* elevated to a main attraction. Even the scaled-down Dh330 menu qualifies as a feast, so make an evening of it – and tomorrow you can take classes here to learn how it's done. Alcohol served.

🍽 MARRAKESH KORNER *Moroccan* $
☎ 0524 389927; 93 Arset Aouzal, near Rue Dar el-Bacha; ⏲ 11am-10.30pm; 📶

Finally, an à la carte menu that's easy on the wallet and kind to the tastebuds. Grab a stool on the cheerful red, yellow and blue rooftop and tuck into a *merguez* sausage sandwich or garlicky courgette salad in the sunshine, or settle into a cushioned corner in the salon for restorative *verveine* tea infusions and free wi-fi. Unless you have a Moroccan grandma, this is the place for classic Friday couscous, properly fluffy and infused with fragrant *smen* (seasoned clarified butter). The hip young staff will encourage you to hang out, sing along to Moroccan pop, and come back often.

🍽 RIAD 72 *Moroccan* $$
☎ 0524 387629; www.riad72.com; Riad 72, 72 Arest Awzel; ⏲ lunch, dinner by reservation; V
Like a model with insane metabolism, this slinky Italian-run guesthouse has a passion for refined homestyle Moroccan dishes. The eggplant caviar makes Beluga seem unoriginal, and potatoes are transformed by a tangy herbal treatment that might make a great facial, too. Go for lunch around the incense-wafting courtyard fountain – the incense can be put out if it's cramping your culinary style – or book ahead for dinner atop the highest terrace around. Alcohol served.

🍸 DRINK

🍸 LA MAISON ARABE BAR *Bar*

☎ 0524 387010; www.lamaisonarabe
.com; 1 Derb Assehbe; ⏰ 8pm-1am; 🚻

It could be the 20-year single malt scotch talking, but fellow drinkers tend to look dashing within these torch-lit leather walls, and the house pianist's Arabic rendition of 'Mack the Knife' is catchy. The fusion tapas are deep-fried beyond all recognition and cocktails hover around Dh100, but never mind: stick to whiskey and hum along.

⭐ PLAY

⭐ HAMMAM BAB DOUKKALA *Hammam*

Rue Bab Doukkala, northeast corner Bab Doukkala Mosque; admission Dh10; ⏰ women noon-7pm, men from 8pm

A simple, lovely community hammam that dates from the 17th century. Pass through the cedar-wood changing room and you'll reach the inner sanctum; here light filters through star-shaped holes in the dome, steam rises from the floor, and the mostly local patrons rest against stately columns while waiting for a *gommage* (body scrub) exfoliating treatment.

⭐ HAMMAM DAR EL-BACHA *Hammam*

20 Rue Fatima Zohra; admission Dh10; ⏰ men 7am-1pm, women 1-9pm

The city's most historic public hammam has domed ceilings so high you'll wonder how the place ever steams up – and yet it has for over a century. A massage costs from Dh50 to Dh100, and *gommage* just Dh15. If the skin-sloughing ever approaches the blood-vessel-breaking point, just say, *'Shwiyya shwiyya'* ('Easy does it'). Bring your public hammam kit (see p143) including dry undies.

⭐ MAISON ARABE *Hammam*

☎ 0524 387010; www.lamaisonarabe
.com; La Maison Arabe Riad, 1 Derb Assehbe; 🅿

Slip into something more comfortable, like this snug *tadelakt* (polished plaster) hammam with vaulted ceilings and baths deliciously scented with local herbs and minerals instead of cloying floral scents. The hammam comes with *gommage* and *rhassoul* (mud scalp rub; Dh350) and hair removal is done here the time-honoured way, with thread and some very fast hands.

> MOUASSINE

At least 500 years old, and yet it hasn't aged a day. The Mouassine reveals traces of ancient Marrakesh in its stately riads, mosques and neighbourhood fountain, yet it stays current with cutting-edge design and cosmopolitan cuisine. This is an ideal place to stay in a riad, given the large number of historic homes in the neighbourhood and its location near the Djemaa el-Fna, souqs and taxis to Nouvelle Ville. Because it's so central and busy, it's safe and easy to navigate for women and solo travellers – yet there's still plenty to discover. Spend a morning exploring Mouassine souqs and *fondouqs* (ancient artisans' studio complexes), where you might glimpse innovative designs destined for the Mouassine's stylish boutiques. The Mouassine offers prices that beat Nouvelle Ville for well-crafted, original lamps, handbags, jewellery and carpets. Chill out between shops in courtyard cafes, and dine in style at your riad or some of the city's best Moroccan restaurants.

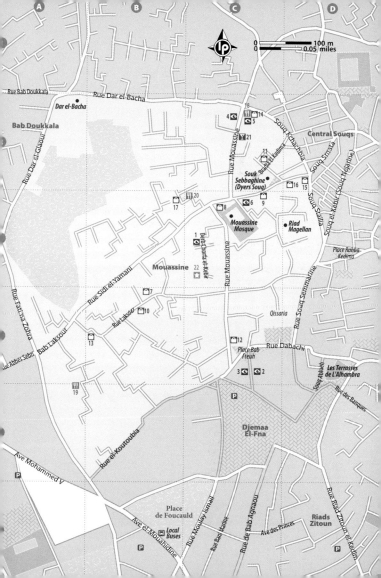

SEE

◉ DAR CHÉRIFA

☎ 0524 426463; www.marrakech-riads
.net; 8 Derb Chorfa Lakbir; admission
free, tea & coffee Dh20-25; ⏰ noon-7pm

Revive souq-sore eyes with a
visit to this serene, impeccably
restored late-15th-century
Saadian riad, where tea and coffee
is served with contemporary art
and literature. Stop by for shows
by local artists, lovely illustrated
editions of Arabic poetry in French
translation, and saffron tea on
the rooftop terrace. Don't miss
concerts and art openings at this
cultural centre, or you'll be left
wandering the streets wondering
where everyone else went.

◉ FONDOUQS

off Djemaa el-Fna, near Place Bab Fteuh
& 196 Rue el-Mouassine, near Café Arabe;
⏰ usually 9am-7pm, individual artisan's
studios vary

Since medieval times, these creative courtyard complexes
featured ground-floor artisans'
workshops and rented rooms

Wood carvings above the Mouassine Fountain (opposite)

upstairs – and from this flux of artisans and adventurers emerged the inventive culture of modern-day Marrakesh. Only 140 *fondouqs* remain in the Medina, including notable ones near Place Bab Ftueh and one on Rue el-Mouassine featured in the film *Hideous Kinky*. The king recently announced a Dh40 million plan to spruce up 98 *fondouqs,* so now's the time to see them in all their shop-worn glory.

MOUASSINE FOUNTAIN

Rue Sidi el-Yamani, near Rue el-Mouassine
The Medina had 80 fountains at the start of the 20th century, and each neighbourhood relied on its own for water for cooking, public baths, orchards and gardens. The Mouassine Fountain is a classic example, with carved wood details and continued use as a neigh-bourhood wool-drying area and gossip source.

SHOP

AL KAWTAR
Moroccan Crafts, Housewares
☎ 0524 378293; www.alkawtar.org; **Rue Laksour 57;** ⏰ 10am-6pm
A smart nonprofit boutique show-casing luxe, minutely embroidered household linens, silk shawls, and fabulous hand-stitched Marrakesh-mod tunics for men, women and kids – no extra charge for alterations. All items here are made by disabled local women, and purchases pay for their salaries, training programs and a childcare centre.

ASSOUSS COOPERATIVE D'ARGANE
Gourmet & Beauty Products
cnr Rue el-Mouassine & Rue Sidi el-Yamani; ⏰ 9am-1pm & 3-7pm Sat-Thu, 9am-noon Fri
Argan oil is the most effective cos-metic and tasty gourmet treat ever to pass through the business end of a goat, and it's the speciality of this women's cooperative. Get yours pure and straight from the source at this women-run shop, and reward artisanal producers for tough work sorting argan pits from goat dung, cracking the rock-hard pits open, and pressing oil from the nut. The richly emollient end product has long protected Sahara-exposed skin, and now European cosmetics companies use it as the secret botanical ingre-dient in high-end creams.

ATELIER MORO
Moroccan Crafts, Fashion
☎ 0524 391678; **114 Place de la Fontaine, near Mouassine Fountain;** ⏰ 10am-1pm & 3-7pm Mon & Wed-Sun
Take the ultimate Marrakesh fashion dare: find the green door by the Mouassine Fountain, ring the doorbell, and head up narrow

V

NEIGHBOURHOODS

MOUASSINE

stairs. Enter at your own budget-ary risk – Marrakesh's top-secret style showcase features entrancing cotton shifts embroidered with good-luck symbols, Lalla Mika's whimsical pom-pom necklaces made from recycled plastic bags, and graphic red-and-white slippers more arresting than stop signs.

CHEZ ADIL *Moroccan Crafts*
☎ 0676 045233; 18 Rue Laksour; ☷ 10am-6.30pm Sat-Thu
Tea-time gets hip at this out-let of hand-thrown Marrakshi designer ceramics in dramatic shapes and appetising colours:

Salah explains Berber symbols at Chez les Nomades (right)

dromedary-humped tangerine teapots, chubby cherry sugar bowls, volcano-shaped creamers in glossy, molten chocolate. You'll recognise iconic Moroccan shapes too – miniature saffron tagines, mint-green crockery tea-glasses, even an octagonal ceramic tea-table in aubergine. Prices are fair enough as quoted, but with gentle bargaining, Adil will probably cut you a deal on larger purchases.

CHEZ LES NOMADES *Carpets*
☎ 0524 442259; www.chezlesnomades.com; 32-34 Bradia El Kedima, near Souq Sebbaghine (Dyers' Souq); ☷ 8.30am-7.30pm
A wide selection of antique and modern Berber carpets, rea-sonable prices, and a pleasant all-round carpet-shopping experi-ence. Multilingual staff will explain with minimal embellishment the key differences, regions and qual-ity with a variety of carpet types, then pull out carpets in whatever style and size appeals to you. Enjoy the tea and the education, without the usual hustle; here the selection speaks for itself.

FONDOUQ OUARZAZI *Moroccan Crafts, Jewellery*
Bab Fteuh square; ☷ most shops 10am-7pm Sat-Thu
Why comb the souqs for silver statement jewellery when you

Mohamed Nour
Geologist turned eco-savvy adventure tour guide and owner of Riad Bledna (p133)

Berber social graces Don't be shy about visiting Berber villages around Marrakesh – they need attention and would really benefit from your visit. Accept invitations to tea, and when you do say *'b'sahaoura'* ('health and rest') and make a slurping noise when you drink – it's actually considered polite. **Tashelhit basics** *'Mament kadgheet?'* means 'How are you doing?' You can answer *'Thinna'*, 'Everything's at peace'. If you see someone in a dry place, it's polite to stop and offer water: *'Bgheetee treet aman?'* **Marrakesh myths** We still use donkeys for transport – they're very green-friendly, you know – but we've got the internet here too. **Great escapes** Everyone needs a break from Marrakesh eventually. One night away is enough to go to the Agafay Desert, the High Atlas mountains, and visit Berber villages in a hidden valley oasis. With another day, you could visit the desert kasbah – often used in movies – at Aït Benhaddou, or Pasha Glaoui's kasbah in the Telouet mountain pass. In three or f   ays, you could trek in Sahara dunes.

can buy straight from the source? This ancient *fondouq* specialises in silver, sold wholesale by weight – though bargaining helps. Don't miss the shops upstairs, where you'll find sand-worn Saharan collars and striking Tuareg silver and leather amulets.

KIFKIF
Accessories, Housewares
☎ 0661 082041; www.kifkifbystef .com; 8 Rue Laksour, near Bab Ksour; ⏱ 10am-8pm

Mirrors made of Moroccan sardine cans, silver rings with interchangeable felt baubles and kids' pyjamas embroidered with 'good night' in Arabic: Kifkif employs Marrakesh's hippest artisans to create original designs often copied but never quite equalled elsewhere. Fifteen per cent of sales of kids' items goes to a local nonprofit children's organisation.

LALLA *Accessories*
www.lalla.fr; 45 Souq Cherifa, near Rue Dar el-Bacha; ⏱ 10am-6pm Mon-Sat

Style trendsetters should count on a late lunch if they make a pitstop at this 1st-floor handbag boutique en route upstairs to Terrasse des Épices (p103). Lalla may be closet-sized, but it's jammed with Marrakesh rocker-chic alternatives to standard-issue Parisian

It bags: studded, low-slung purple totes, retro-'70s tapestry catch-alls made of vintage Moroccan upholstery fabrics, buckled hobo-bags in buttery leather the exact shade of *smen* (seasoned butter).

L'ART DU BAIN SAVONNERIE ARTISANALE
Beauty Products
☎ 0668 445942; www.lartdubain.net; Souq Lebbadine, near Souq Sebbaghine; ⏱ 10am-7pm Mon-Sat

An abundance of fragrant, artisanal bath products delight the senses: pyramids of handmade palm oil soaps with organic bergamot and vetiver; towers of shaving soap with soothing Moroccan mint; and shelves of argan oil from an Essaouira cooperative, in tassel-topped bottles. Organic, artisanal soaps cost just Dh30 to Dh50 (fixed price), and gifts come sprinkled with rosebuds and star anise and tied with raffia.

MASROURE ABDILLAH
Accessories, Moroccan Crafts
☎ 0664 817254; 53 Souq Lebbadine, near Souq Sebbaghine; ⏱ 9am-7.30pm

It usually takes decades to earn the title *maâlem* (master craftsperson), but young Masroure earns the title the hard way, pounding wool with *savon noir* (black soap) into felt. He then moulds it into seamless slippers, baubles for necklaces, and sturdy tote bags. Masroure's felt flowers come in snappy shades of natural brown, bright orange and splashy hot pink, and make groovy brooches, hatpins and everlasting bouquets.

🏠 MINISTERO DEL GUSTO
Art, Housewares, Fashion

☎ 0524 426455; www.ministerodel gusto.com; Derb Azzouz, off Rue Sidi el-Yamani, near Rue el-Mouassine; ⏰ 10am-1pm Mon-Sat, afternoons by appointment

You may have to elbow David Bowie and Iman out of the way to snap up that Moroccan pop art painting. Stop by to ogle the Gaudí-gone-Berber decor, and score custom-designed accessories such as hand-carved lemonwood cutlery plus vintage finds – including some killer vintage party dresses on the mezzanine. Call ahead, or you might find the place closed for a fashion mag photo shoot.

🍴 EAT
🍴 TERRASSE DES ÉPICES
Moroccan, Mediterranean $$

☎ 0524 375904; www.terrassedesepices .com; 15 Souq Cherifia, off Rue Dar el-Bacha; ⏰ noon-11pm

Head to the roof for lunch on top of the world in a mudbrick *bhou* (booth). Check out the chalkboard for daily à la carte specials, which typically include dinner-sized Caesar salads, flaky *bastilla* with chicken or traditional pigeon, and vegetarian aubergine pasta with thyme. Save room for house-speciality chocolate *bastilla,* layers of *warqa* pastry, apricots, prunes and almonds smothered in chocolate. Reserve ahead during high season; cards are accepted, but no alcohol is served.

🍴 TOBSIL
Moroccan Fixed-price Feast $$$

☎ 0524 441523; 22 Derb Moulay Abdellah ben Hessaien, near Bab Laksour; ⏰ 7.30-11pm Wed-Mon, reservations required

Dar Moha and Al Fassia have the edge for à la carte menus, but Tobsil is a date-night draw for decadent feasts in an intimate riad. As Gnaoua musicians play in the courtyard, up to 50 guests (no tour groups here) indulge in button-popping five-course menus with aperitifs and wine for Dh650. No excess glitz and belly dancers distract from upstanding *meze* (starters), *bastilla* (pigeon pie), tagines (yes, that's plural) and couscous, capped off with mint tea, fresh fruit and Moroccan pastries.

The art of tea at Dar Chérifa's literary cafe (p98)

🔲 VILLA FLORE
Moroccan Fusion $$

☎ 0524 391700; www.villa-flore.com; 4 Derb Azzouz; 🕒 12.30-3pm & 7.30-11pm Wed-Mon

Some come for meltingly tender lamb and duck; some for the relaxed black-and-white riad setting that's snazzy as a tuxedo and comfy as a *djellaba*; and others, it must be admitted, for that blindingly handsome maitre d'. But the best draw is the Dh60 Moroccan salads: three perfect circles of Moroccan *meze* that elevate lowly

aubergines and peppers to major sensations with aromatic *ras al-hanout* spice.

🍸 DRINK

🍸 CAFÉ ARABE *Cafe-Bar*

☎ 0524 429728; www.cafearabe.com; 184 Rue el-Mouassine; 🕒 9am-midnight; ♿ 🅥 👶

Gloat over souq purchases with cocktails on the roof or alongside the Zen-*zellij* (mosaic) courtyard fountain. Wine prices here are down to earth for such a stylish place, and you can order half-bottles of better Moroccan wines such as the peppery red Siroua S. The food is bland but the company isn't – artists and designers flock here – so grab a bite and join the conversation.

⭐ PLAY

⭐ **LE BAIN BLEU** *Hammam*
☎ **0524 426999; www.lebainbleu.com; 32 Derb Chorfa Lakbir, near Rue Mouassine;** 🕑 **10am-9pm by appointment**

This spiffy new riad spa-hammam delivers top-notch style and value in a top-secret location. Follow the signs for Dar Cherifa off Rue Mouassine onto Derb Chorfa, then keep heading south to this double riad with sunny, secluded patios, sleek subterranean steam rooms and a range of relaxing, professional spa treatments (massages Dh350 per hour, hammam and *gommage* Dh150, couples hammam and massage Dh600 per person, manicure or pedicure Dh280).

> RIADS ZITOUN & KASBAH

Ultramodern and ancient are never far apart in Marrakesh, as you'll discover when you bunk in among the monuments at a trendy local riad, get the latest spa treatments at a Kasbah hammam or troll boutiques for original designs along Rue Riad Zitoun el-Kedim. Visitors emerge dazed from neighbourhood *derbs* (winding alleys), gobsmacked by riads and palaces that are floor-to-ceiling showplaces of Marrakshi creativity. To the east of Riad Zitoun el-Jedid are three marvellous Marrakesh mansions: the elegantly refined Dar Si Said, now a museum that shows how Moroccans make an art of everyday life, from doorknobs to daggers; Maison Tiskiwin, home and living history museum of anthropologist Bert Flint; and Bahia Palace, where harems once held court and Mohammed VI still holds royal parties for rappers. Near the Bahia Palace is the Mellah, once the largest Jewish quarter in North Africa. With 20th-century emigration to Europe, the neighbourhood became mostly Muslim, and it's now called Hay-Es-Salam – but the neighbourhood's ancient character remains, as do its myriad contributions to Marrakshi society, craft and commerce.

RIADS ZITOUN & KASBAH

SEE

AGDAL GARDENS

south of the Royal Palace, Kasbah;
3-6.30pm Fri, noon-6pm Sun
Moroccan sultans have greeted
dignitaries here for eight centuries, among fragrant fruit and
olive orchards and reflecting pools
stocked with psychic carp that
sense you and your bread crusts
coming. The gardens still serve
ceremonial purposes, so they're
only open weekends and when
the king isn't in residence.

BAB AGNAOU

exterior of Medina ramparts, 20m north
of Bab er-Rob
One of the 20 gates in the Marrakesh city walls, this 12th-century
'gate of the Gnaoua' (named for
the sub-Saharan slaves who served
the sultan) was one of the first
stone monuments in Marrakesh
and a triumph of Marrakshi artisan-
ship. From afar the bas-relief ap-
pears much deeper than it actually
is, due to a sophisticated trompe
l'oeil effect. The bluish-gold-green
colour of its Guéliz stone seems to
change like a mood ring according
to the time of the day, the heat
and, perhaps, the city's disposition.

BADI PALACE

near Place des Ferblantiers;
admission Dh10, incl Koutobia Minbar
Dh20; 9am-4.30pm

When 16th-century Sultan Ahmed
el-Mansour was paving his palace
with gold, turquoise and crystal,
his jester wisecracked, 'It'll make
a beautiful ruin'. That fool was a
prophet: 75 years later the place
was looted. Hard to picture the
former glories of the now-barren
courtyard, and the next-door
garden is a royal mess with the
king's security equipment – but
the stork's-eye view atop the
ramparts and periodic concerts
here are musts.

BAHIA PALACE

0524 389564; Rue Riad Zitoun
el-Jedid; admission Dh10; 9am-
4.30pm;
Modern special-effects wizardry
can't beat the optical effects of
intricate stucco work and polychrome *zellij* (mosaic) topped by
painted, inlaid woodwork ceilings.
It took 14 years to achieve this
effect in the late 19th century,
and you can picture the intrigues
that unfolded here back then:
subjects pleading for clemency in
the Court d'Honneur; courtesans
courting pashas' attentions in
romantic gardens or hiding from
them in private harem nooks; and
enemies and wives of the Grand
Vizier stripping the palace bare
of its opulent furnishings before
his body was cold. The entrance
is near Place des Ferblantiers. See
p17 for more.

Bab Agnaou (left) is one of 20 gates in the Marrakesh city walls

☉ DAR SI SAID
☎ 0524 389564; Rue Kennaria, near Rue Riad Zitoun el-Jedid; admission Dh30; ⏰ 9am-4.30pm; ♿

A monument to Moroccan *maâlems* (master craftsmen), the Dar Si Said highlights Marrakesh's graceful riad architecture and local craftsmanship – though artisans from Fez must be credited for the spectacular painted woodwork in the domed wedding chamber upstairs. Don't miss the door collection on the ground floor, painted musicians' balconies on the first,

and displays of opulent silk velvet kaftans. Tempting though it may be, no photographing or touching the displays is allowed. See p20 for more.

☉ KOUTOUBIA MINBAR
Badi Palace; admission Dh20 incl Badi Palace; ⏰ 9am-4.30pm

Not to be confused with an ordinary staircase or a hotel beverage dispensary, this minbar (pulpit) is the Koutoubia's 12th-century prayer pulpit. With intricately carved cedar wood steps and

NEIGHBOURHOODS

RIADS ZITOUN & KASBAH

minute gold, silver and ivory marquetry, this minbar is a credit to Cordoban craftsmanship under Moroccan rule and *maâlem* Aziz – the Metropolitan Museum of Art restoration uncovered his signature under the inlay.

MAISON TISKIWIN
☎ 0524 389192; www.tiskiwin.com;
8 Rue de la Bahia; adult/child Dh20/10;
🕑 9.30am-12.30pm & 2.30-6pm

Travel to Timbuktu and back again, via the private art collection of Dutch anthropologist Bert Flint. Each room represents a region of Morocco with indigenous crafts, from well-travelled Tuareg leather camel saddles to fine Middle Atlas carpets – the gold standard by which to judge the ones in the souqs. See if you can spot such recurring motifs as the *khamsa* (hand of Fatima) and the Southern

Chamber of the Three Niches, Saadian Tombs (right)

cross, the constellation that guided desert travellers.

MELLAH

east on Rue Riad Zitoun el-Jedid, south of the Bahia Palace
In the narrow *derbs* of the city's historic Jewish quarter are the tallest mudbrick buildings in Marrakesh, with cross-alley chats in progress through wrought-iron Mellah balconies. Some doors are embellished with six-pointed stars and menorahs, and you may be guided towards the local synagogue and the Miaâra (Jewish Cemetery), where guardians request donations from visitors for upkeep. But to see the living legacy of Mellah artisans and spice traders, check out the Place des Ferblantiers, Grand Bijouterie and Mellah Market.

SAADIAN TOMBS

Rue de la Kasbah, near Kasbah Mosque; admission Dh10; 9am-4.45pm;
Elvis Presley's tastes seem restrained compared with those of Sultan Ahmed al-Mansour, who spared no expense on his tomb, importing Italian Carrara marble and gilding honeycomb *muqarnas* (stalactite-type stone carving) archways with pure gold. The sultan played favourites even in death, keeping princes handy in the Chamber of the Three Niches, and relegating to garden plots chancellors and wives – all of

which are overshadowed by his mother's splendid mausoleum. See p15 for more.

SHOP

ARANTXA MUÑOZ *Fashion*

53 Riad Zitoun el-Jedid; www.arantxa munoz.com; 10am-7pm Sat-Thu
Easygoing, cosmopolitan Marrakshi style, with a souq sense of humour: tunic dresses with punky studded collars, cheerfully apolitical rainbow-coloured *kaffiyas* (woven scarves), black and white wing-tip style ballet flats handmade from soft Moroccan kid leather, and totes made of orange African status cloth printed with blue Euro notes.

AYA'S *Fashion*

** 0524 383428; www.ayasmarrakech .com; 11bis Derb Jedid Bab Mellah; 9.30am-1pm & 3-7pm Mon-Thu & Sat, 3-7pm Fri**
Deluxe, hand-embroidered designer fashions worthy of a royal reception are offered here, from chocolate brown linen tunics with geometric, sky-blue embroidery to striped-silk kaftans in jewel tones straight out of a Matisse painting. Men's offerings include sleek navy brushed-wool jackets and linen shirts with hand-knotted silk buttons. They're not cheap, but they don't cost a king's ransom, either – and alterations are gratis.

NEIGHBOURHOODS

RIADS ZITOUN & KASBAH

🏠 BIJOUTERIE EL-YASMINE
Jewellery
68 Rue Riad Zitoun el-Jedid;
🕐 **10am-7pm**
Yasmin's simplified takes on traditional motifs look (and cost) like
adornments instead of dowry pay-
ments. Check out hammered silver
teaspoons with striped ebony and
enamel handles, lucky turquoise
enamel hand-of-Fatima earrings,
and Tuareg-inspired cocktail rings
that look like hypnotist's props
with concentric circles in dark
wood and bright orange enamel.

🏠 CREATIONS PNEUMATIQUES
Housewares, Moroccan Crafts
☎ **0666 091746; 110-111 Rue Riad
Zitoun el-Kedim;** 🕐 **10am-7pm**
Atlas Abdelghani is a Bob Marley
fan, as you can see from the
posters he's framed with recycled
tyres, with one word embedded
over Marley's head: 'Michelin'. This
is one recycling *maâlem* with a
sneaky sense of humour and
serious ingenuity; crafts range
from treasure chests with air
valves as drawer pulls to tyre-tread
flip-flops with serious traction.

🏠 GNAOUA MUSIC SHOP
Musical Instruments
84 Rue Riad Zitoun el-Jedid;
🕐 **10am-8pm**
You'll have to duck to avoid banging the drums over the doorway

with your head, but you've come
to the right place to go Gnaoua
and join a jam session. These are
the handmade, rustic instruments
played in the Djemaa el-Fna, from
recycled-metal castanets to goat-
skins stretched over sturdy frames
that can take a real pounding.

🏠 GRAND BIJOUTERIE
Jewellery
**Rue Bab Mellah, opposite entrance to
Bahia Palace;** 🕐 **9.30am-8pm**
Get reeled in by small silver
charms, and hooked by gold
chandelier earrings that tickle
shoulders and deplete bank reserves. Pieces are sold by weight,
so serious shoppers should know
the going market rate for gold
and silver and mind the scales.
The fancy filigree jewellery hails
from India, but you'll still spy
some local jewellers diligently
plying their trade.

🏠 JAMADE
Housewares, Moroccan Crafts
☎ **0524 429042; 1 Place Douar Graoua,
off Rue Riad Zitoun el-Jedid;** 🕐 **10am-
noon & 3-7pm Sat-Thu**
As you might guess from Jamade's
deep-purple floor and space-age
orange ceramic tea sets, this is not
your granny's idea of a Moroccan
crafts shop. The stock is stylish
and prices are fixed; featured local
designs include coasters embroi-

MY, AREN'T YOU THOUGHTFUL

By bringing these Marrakshi treats to friends back home, you're also promoting fair trade, worthy causes and recycling in Marrakesh:

> Fashion and hand-carved thuya wood boxes from Cooperative Artisanale Femmes de Marrakech (p84)
> Argan oil from Assouss Cooperative D'Argane (p99)
> Tigmi embroidered coasters from Jamade (opposite) and KifKif (p102) embroidered children's pyjamas with proceeds supporting children's nonprofit organisations
> Linens embroidered with lucky Berber motifs at Al Kawtar (p99), a nonprofit centre for disabled women
> Recycled tyre crafts from Creations Pneumatiques (opposite) and sardine-tin home decor from Kifkif (p102)

dered with Berber *baraka* (good vibes) by Tigmi women's cooperative and perfumes blended from indigenous plants by Héritage Berbère.

🏠 KASBEK/CHEZ AMAL & TIFTIF *Fashion*
☎ 0662 489485; 216 Riad Zitoun el-Jedid; 🕑 10am-7pm Sat-Thu
Tiftif searches the Sahara for polished cotton jacquard in sumptuous jewel tones, and Amal fashions it into ingenious fashions that flatter womanly shapes, yet magically leave room for more couscous. Get dresses tailor-made or tunics off the rack with Berber power symbols embroidered on the back.

🏠 MADEMOISELLE IBTISSAM'S ORIGINAL DESIGN *Housewares*
☎ 0524 380361; www.original-design -mrk.com; 47 Place des Ferblantiers,

near Badi Palace; 🕑 9.30am-12.30pm & 2.30-7.30pm
With handcrafted table accessories this glamorous, you could order takeaway and still wow your guests: rocket ship–red tagine presentation dishes, linen tablecloths with playful pompoms, twin mini-tagines for salt and pepper, tasselled silk napkin holders and more. The fixed prices are already a bargain.

🏠 MELLAH MARKET *Food Market*
Ave Houmane el-Fetouaki, near Place des Ferblantiers; 🕑 8am-1pm & 3-7pm
For the south side of the city, this is a major source for food, flowers and other household goods. Fair warning to vegetarians: the door closest to Place des Ferblantiers leads directly to the chicken and meat area.

RIADS ZITOUN & KASBAH

⬜ WARDA LA MOUCHE
Fashion
☎ 0524 472088; 1 Derb Sidi Boulafdaiel;
🕙 9.30am-9pm Tue-Sun

This local designer makes glamour look easy with embroidered tunic T-shirts, metal-embroidered kaftans and psychedelic slippers. Prices are fixed, and about what you'd pay for mass-produced basics back home.

🍴 EAT

🍴 MAMA TILEE *Fusion* $$
☎ 0524 381752; www.mamatilee.blog spot.com; 13 Derb Laarsa, off Riad Zitoun el-Jedid; 🕙 7.30pm-11pm Mon-Sat

Only 22 diners nightly are treated to Chef Cecile's three-course *prix-fixe* (Dh220) starring organic local ingredients in this sleek riad restaurant. The menu is strictly seasonal, with inspired choices: mango gazpacho or foie gras with fig for starters, sole roulade with kaffir lime or steak with High Atlas herbs as mains, and finally, passionfruit crème brûlée or Moroccan mint-chocolate *macarons*. Reserve by phone in afternoons; cash only, alcohol licence pending.

🍴 NID' CIGOGNE
Sandwiches, Snacks $
☎ 0524 382092; 60 Place des Tombeaux Saadians; 🕙 9am-9pm

This rooftop restaurant lets you get up close and personal with

the storks across the way at the Saadian Tombs, and offers service-able grilled *kefta* (spiced meatball) sandwiches and light salads, and nothing-special tagines. Service is slow, but pleasant considering those steep stairs.

🍴 RESTAURANT PLACE DES FERBLANTIERS
Moroccan à la Carte $
west entrance Place des Ferblantiers, near Mellah Market

For a quick, tasty tagine served bubbling hot right off the burner, look no more at touristy palace restaurants with plodding service. Plop down on a plastic chair in the courtyard, and have whatever's freshest that day – the meat and produce come from the Mellah Market across the street, and you can see the cook whipping up tagines right in front of you.

🍴 RYAD JANA
Moroccan à la Carte $
☎ 0524 429872; 149 Rue Kennaria, off Riad Zitoun el-Jedid

Finally, a family-run riad restau-rant that serves à la carte lunches at realistic prices, along with generous helpings of Moroccan hospitality. Enjoy your lamb tag-ine with prunes and almonds in the restful garden for only slightly more than you'd pay to dine on a skimpy version in the dusty Djemaa, and win huge accolades for trying even a few words of Moroccan Arabic.

UN DEJEUNER À MARRAKESH

Sandwiches, Pastries $

☎ 0524 378387; 2-4 Rue Kennaria, cnr Rue Riad Zitoun el-Jedid; ⏱ 9am-5pm; V

Come early, or forfeit flaky, just-baked quiche of the day with asparagus or courgettes to ravenous vegetarians. Omnivores practically pig out on decadent *croque-monsieurs* (toasted ham-and-cheese sandwiches) made with turkey, served with side salads in a tangy herb-spiked lime dressing. Stick to comfy ground-floor booths for prompt attention to your urgent coffee needs by the attentive all-women staff. The sunny, tented terrace three floors up has pillows strewn around low tables and prime Koutoubia views, but understandably slower, less chipper service.

DRINK

KOSYBAR *Bar*

☎ 024 380324; http://kozibar.tripod .com; 47 Place des Ferblantiers; ⏱ noon-1am;

The Marrakesh-meets-Kyoto interiors are plenty fabulous, with 19th-century *zellij* bumping up against Shinto-shrine exposed beams, but you'd be wise to skip the less-than-inspired sushi and head straight up to the roof terrace bar overlooking the Badi Palace. Here Moroccan wines are served with a side of samba, and storks give you the once-over from nearby nests.

PLAY

DAR ES-SALAM *Cabaret*

☎ 0524 443520; www.daressalam.com; 170 Rue Riad Zitoun el-Kedim; ⏱ 7-11pm

This restaurant was featured in Hitchcock's *The Man Who Knew Too Much*, and it still specialises in surprise endings. The unexpected twist comes around 9pm, when a woman in a spangled unitard emerges bearing a tray of lit candles on her head and proceeds to perform callisthenic dance manoeuvres like a pyromaniac Romanian gymnast. But the night will not be over until the final twist – the Berber band breaks into a rousing bar-mitzvah chorus of 'Hava Nagila'.

RIAD SPA BAHIA SALAM *Hammam*

☎ 0524 426060; 61 Ave Houmane el-Fetouaki, near Rue de Bab Agnaou; ⏱ 9am-7pm

Shiny new spa facilities in a converted riad leave visitors fresh and dewy as the roses at the Mellah Market across the street. In addition to traditional treatments such as hammam and *gommage* (Dh200 per person) and *takssila* (gentle, passive stretching by a massage therapist, like a lazy version of yoga), individuals and couples can unwind with Jacuzzi and sauna access, thyme-lavender scrubs (Dh150), and hamman, body wrap and massage package deals (from Dh400 per person).

⭐ **SULTANA SPA** *Hammam*
☎ 0524 388008; www.lasultanamarra kech.com; Rue de la Kasbah, next to Saadian Tombs; Ⓟ
Through the majestic archways lies this glistening marble spa, its glowing emerald pool flanked by private cabins for gentle *gommage* treatments with organic plant extracts and essential oils (€25). Get the royal treatment with two- or four-handed amber-oil massages (two-handed €45 per 50 minutes, four-handed €50 per 30 minutes) in a roof-terrace pavilion.

Drift off on a boat-bed at Riad Enija (p128)

RIADS

Paris has its cathedrals, New York its skyscrapers, but riads are what set Marrakesh apart. These spectacular mudbrick courtyard mansions are oases of calm in the bustling Medina: push through the brass-studded wooden doors and suddenly you're in a courtyard lined with soaring Moorish arches and cozy *bhous* (seating nooks). Metre-thick mudbrick walls block out street noise, so that when the door closes on the hubbub of the souqs you can hear burbling courtyard fountains and songbirds in pomegranate trees. Behind its pink walls Marrakesh has more authentic riads than any other city in North Africa, and they include exuberantly ornamented examples from the 17th century.

Over the past decade, hundreds of these historic family homes have been sold and reinvented as guesthouses, mainly by Europeans. The best are not just marvels of the Marrakshi tradition of craftsmanship – which guesthouses helped revive – but unforgettable experiences of Marrakshi hospitality, complete with insights into the local culture and shifting social mores. 'Riad' is now a synonym for guesthouse, and the ones highlighted in this chapter offer a range of must-have Marrakshi experiences: made-to-order Moroccan feasts from an ingenious *dada* (cook); hammam treatments; courses on everything from cooking to mosaics taught by a *maâlem* (expert craftsperson); and excursions to mountain villages and the Sahara beyond. Staying in a riad isn't just about sleeping in posh digs; it's about gaining an understanding of Marrakesh behind those studded doors. For information on accommodation outside the Medina, see p132.

RIADS

A

20 Arset Ihiri

R. Koutoubia
R. kala

12 Rue el-Gaza

Derb Jedid

16

Rue Fatima Zohra

Derb (Hotel) **25**

Derb Dekkak

17 **29**

Mosque
Arset Awzel
8 R. Bab Doukkala
14

BAB DOUKKALA

Derb Asehbe

B

Rue el-Gaza

DAR EL-BACHA

2

Derb Halfaoui

23

13

Rue Dar el-Bacha

Rue Dar el-Glaoui

MOUASSINE

Derb
el-Hammam

1

4

9

Rue Sidi el-Yamani

R. el Ksour

Rue el-Mouassine

Rue el-Koutoubia

Rue Fatima Zohra

Ave Mohammed V

R. Abbes Sebti

Place de
Foucauld
Ave el-Mouahidine

Ave Houmane el-Fetouaki

R. Sidi Mimoun

Bab
el-Jedid

Blvd el-Yarmouk

Olive
Groves

Bab Agnaou
Cemetery

C

Rue el-Assouel

MEDINA

5

Rue Riad
Laarauss

Place be
Youssef

Kaarhen a'kbir

CENTRAL
SOUQS

27

Place Rahba
Qedima

21 **30**

Derb Moulay
Abdelkader

Qissaria

Place
Bab Fteuh

19

Rue Debachi

Derb Jdid

DJEMAA
EL-FNA

7

Rue de Bab Agnaou

26

Rue Riad Zitoun el-Jedid

Derb Jedid

24

18

Ave Houmane el-Fetouaki

Rue Riad Zitoun el-Kedim

28

Rue Bab Mellah

Rue Uqba ben Nafaa

Rue Oqba ben Nafaa

Bab
Agnaou

KASBAH

R. de la Kasbah

Derb
Mnabha

10

D

0   200 m
0   0.1 miles

R de Taber Khemis

Derb
Mesfioui

Derb Lalla
Azzouna

3
31 **6**

DERB
DEBACHI

Derb Jdid

22

15

11 Derb Lahbib
Maghni

Miaâra
Jewish
Cemetery

R. de Miaâra

Place
des Ferblantiers

RIADS
ZITOUN

RIADS

RIAD RATES

Rates can vary dramatically depending on the time of year and length of stay – inquire about specials for longer stays and low-season rates via the various riads' websites. Low season is usually summer (mid-June to August) and winter (mid-January to mid-March). Book a month ahead and expect high-season rates during major European holidays (especially Christmas/New Year and Easter/Passover). Mid-season rates cover most of spring and autumn, and are indicated in this chapter as follows, including breakfast:

> \$\$\$ Top End: over Dh1300
> \$\$ Midrange: Dh800-1300
> \$ Budget: under Dh800

MOUASSINE

DAR AL KOUNOUZ   \$
☎ 0524 390773; www.daralkounouz
.com; 54 Derb Snane; ⚄ 🛜 🛁 ♿
The roof terrace overlooks the royal Dar el-Bacha next door, but the real action is downstairs, where you can learn the chef's secrets in the kitchen or be massaged in the marble hammam. Lazy mornings are meant for curling up by the fireplace in the library under the stained-glass cupola. Babysitting available.

DAR ATTAJMIL   \$\$
☎ 0524 426966; www.darattajmil.com;
23 Rue el-ksour; ⚄ 🛜
This riad is rosy and relaxed, and you will be too after a few days within these Marrakshi pink *tadelakt* (polished plaster) walls. Lucrezia and her attentive staff offer a warm welcome and an even warmer rooftop hammam,

plus scrumptious Moroccan-fusion dinners, cooking classes, *zellij* (mosaic) workshops and Essaouira escapes.

DAR MOUASSINE   \$\$
☎ 0524 445287; www.darmouassine
.com; 148 Derb Snane; ⚄ 🛜 🛋 📺
Skip the guitar lessons: against this glam backdrop of mod furnishings, ironwork balconies and original 17th-century doors, anyone looks like a rock star. Stage album cover shoots beside the *tadelakt* pool or in the Jacuzzi, and live large in the Cardamom Suite with its intricate woodwork ceiling and turreted bathroom.

TOP FIVE FOR FOOD
> Jnane Tamsna (p133)
> Maison Mnabha (p122)
> Riad 72 (p126)
> La Maison Arabe (p125)
> Riad Bledna (p133)

LES JARDINS DE MOUASSINE $
☎ 0672 581078; www.lesjardinsdem
ouassine.com; 20 Derb Chorfa el-Kebir;

Recover from shopping fatigue
and forget you're steps away from
Medina souqs in the in-house
hammam, library, lounge, pool,
or sunny terraces across three
interconnected riads. Themed
guestrooms highlight Marra-
keshi artisan specialities – drums,
saddles, slippers – and parents
will appreciate that baby beds are
free, and in-room massages are
available.

RIAD L'ORANGERAIE $$$
☎ 0661 238789; www.riadorangeraie
.com; 61 Rue Sidi el-Yamani;
It's smooth and suave, with
perfectly buffed *tadelakt* walls,
massaging showers (the best in
town), a chlorine-free pool and
sprawling rooms. This place has
all the right moves, with five
employees looking after seven
rooms, a car and driver at your
disposal, excellent breakfasts, a
hammam, ecofriendly products
and in-house recycling.

RIAD MAGELLAN $
☎ 0661 082042; www.riadmagellan
.com; 62 Derb el-Hammam;
World travellers will want to put
down roots in this retro riad,
where steamer trunks, antique

Rock-star style at Dar Mouassine (opposite)

globes and 1930s fans bring back
the cosmopolitan glamour of Art
Deco Marrakesh. A terrace hot tub
and deep-tissue massages soothe
away economy-airfare kinks, and
kindly staff make this well-hidden,
but ideally located, retreat feel like
home.

RIADS ZITOUN & KASBAH

JNANE MOGADOR $

☎ 0524 426324; www.jnanemogador
.com; 116 Derb Sidi Bouloukat, off Rue
Riad Zitoun el-Kedim; 🛜 ♿

The sweetest deal in the souqs:
a prime location, in-house hammam, double-decker roof terraces,
and owner Mohammed's laid-back
hospitality. A favourite with
diplomats and artists; book ahead
and enjoy fascinating breakfast
conversation.

MAISON MNABHA $$

☎ 0524 381325; www.maisonmnabha
.com; 32-3 Derb Mnabha, Kasbah;
❌ 🛜 🖨

Treasure-hunters seek out this
17th-century Kasbah hideaway
brimming with elusive finds. In
antique-filled salons celebrity
chefs, novelists and other regulars
mingle over cocktails and creative
cuisine. English brothers Peter and
Lawrence and manager Aziz are a
wealth of impartial antiques advice
and cultural insight – Peter holds a
PhD in Kasbah history – and
arrange restorative massages,
henna tattooing and eco-conscious
desert adventures.

MARHBABIKOUM $

☎ 0524 375204; www.marhbabikoum
.com; 43 Derb Lahbib Magni; 🖥 ❌ ♿

The name means welcome,
and you'll feel it when you step
through the door. Khalil and
Véronique run their mellow riad
family-style, so you're automati-
cally invited for tea, chats, card
games and Moroccan jam sessions
already in progress. If you can tear

Indulge in creative cuisine amid the antiques at Maison Mnabha (above)

RIADS

TOP FIVE FOR AUTHENTIC MOROCCAN HOSPITALITY

> Dar Tayib (p128)
> Marhbabikoum (opposite)
> Riad Akka (below)
> Jnane Mogador (opposite)
> Riad Kniza (p127)

yourself away, mountain excursions can be arranged.

RIAD AKKA $$$
☎ 0524 375767; www.riad-akka.com; 65 Derb Lahbib Magni;
Heartfelt hospitality meets worldly chic: Arabic sayings about cross-cultural understanding grace the courtyard patio, flowers fill graphite-*tadelakt* guestrooms, homemade tarts appear at teatime, and laid-back French and Moroccan hosts mingle easily with guests. Luxury amenities include a plunge pool, rooftop lounge, in-house hammam, and in-room wi-fi; proceeds support a local staff of five and a Moroccan women's microcredit association.

RIAD EDEN $
☎ 0672 046910; www.riadeden-marrakech.com; 25 Derb Jedid;
Generous cooks, a comfy living room and energetic young French family owners make the Eden a sociable spot. Pull up a chair in

the kitchen and watch culinary magic happen. Families prefer the spacious Cannelle room, while couples request the snug, rooftop Orange room; all rooms are air-conditioned except the ground-floor Berber room.

RIAD IFOULKI $$
☎ 0524 385656; www.riadifoulki.com; 11 Derb Maqadem, Rue Arset Loghzail, Debbachi;
Guests become instant locals at this 300-year-old triple riad in an untouristy neighbourhood east of Djemaa el-Fna, featuring an in-house hammam, candlelit massages and workshops on Marrakesh traditions from Sufism to belly-dancing. Multilingual owner Peter Bergmann is a passionate community advocate – ask about his latest initiative, a Mellah cultural complex.

RIAD KAISS $$$
☎ 0524 440141; www.riadkaiss.com; 65 Derb Jdid, off Riad Zitoun el-Kedim;
Take a look around this palatial double riad: this is why visitors rave about Moroccan craftsmanship. From the mosaic floors to hand-painted ceilings, Kaïss is a tribute to Marrakesh *maâlems* (master craftsmen). But Kaiss has smarts as well as looks, with sharp new management offering

cooking classes, in-house hammam and massages, a private driver and shopping valet services. Step onto private suite balconies overlooking pomegranate trees and fountains, and you'll understand why songbirds flock here for inspiration.

RIAD LES BOUGAINVILLIERS $$$
☎ 0524 391717; www.riadlesbougainvilliers.com; 5 Derb Ben Amrane; ✂ 🖼 👶
Like Prozac, this sunny double riad lifts moods overnight, with soaring archways, exposed brick and natural wood. Suites verge on bland, but junior suite Jasmin and double Jacaranda induce instant harmony. Staff is professional without being stuffy, and arrange arrivals by horse-drawn carriage, massages, babysitting, mountain excursions, cooking classes and weddings.

RIAD NESMA $
☎ 0524 444442; www.riadnesma.com; 128 Riad Zitoun el-Kedim; P ✂ 👶

TOP FIVE FOR CULTURAL EXPERIENCE
> Riad al Massarah (p126)
> Riad Sahara Nour (p127)
> Riyad el Cadi (p129)
> Riad Ifoulki (p123)
> Jnane Tamsna (p133)

For snug rooms styled after different Moroccan dynasties overlooking the souq, Nesma is a bargain. But check out the luxury amenities: in-house hammam and massage, rooftop breakfasts with Badi Palace views, even parking at your doorstep.

BAB DOUKKALA & DAR EL-BACHA
DAR BARAKA & DAR KARAM $
☎ 0524 391609; www.marrakech-riads.net; 18 &11 Derb Halfaoui; ✂ 🛜 👶
High style at low prices, with sharp staff, an in-house hammam and tranquil, whitewashed rooms with authentic period details: arabesque archways, cedar ceilings and polychrome stucco. These conjoined-twin riads are connected by a vast roof terrace, plus a shared fondness for rose petals, lanterns and firm beds.

DAR SOUKAINA $$
☎ 0661 245238; www.darsoukaina.com; 19 Derb el-Ferrane, Riad Laârouss; ✂ 🖼
Fraternal twin riads: the first (Dar I) is all soaring ceilings, cosy nooks and graceful archways, while the spacious double-riad extension (Dar II and III) across the *derb* (alley) offers sprawling beds, grand patios, a plunge pool and handsome woodwork. Omar keeps both

houses running like clockwork and offers reliable insider tips on Marrakesh. A 20-minute walk from the Djemaa and nearest gate, but near parking on Riad Laarous.

LA MAISON ARABE $$$

☎ 0524 387010; www.lamaisonarabe .com; 1 Derb Assehbe;

The legendary restaurant is now a glamorous guesthouse, tastefully outfitted with North African antiques, a yummy restaurant, slinky bar, acclaimed culinary classes and a scrumptious hammam where you can marinate in baths of local herbs and mineral salts.

NOIR D'IVOIRE $$$

☎ 0524 380975; www.noir-d-ivoire .com; 31 Derb Jedid;

The gobsmacking opulence includes a foyer chandelier 4.5m wide and guest mobile phones supplied by English owner/tastemaker Jill Fechtmann. Sink into soft armchairs in the well-stocked library, lounge by the grand

Enjoy the cosmopolitan glamour of Riad Magellan (p121)

RIADS

piano in the leather-clad cocktail bar, and enjoy shiatsu and chocolates by the private spa fireplace. Decadent, but thoughtful too, from the water-conserving filtered pool to organic spa products.

RIAD 12 $$
☎ 0524 387629; www.riad12.com; 12 Derb Sraghnas; ✂ ⬛
The heart-stealing younger sister of Riad 72 (below), with a sunnier disposition, magazine-ready looks, and echoing rooms that would qualify as suites elsewhere. The downside: you'll have to be pried from your butterfly chair by the courtyard pool to take advantage of the excellent meals and hammam at Riad 72.

RIAD 72 $$$
☎ 0524 387629; www.riad72.com; 72 Arset Awzel; ✂ ⬛
Like a kaftan-clad supermodel on a Vespa, the 72 defines jet-set chic. All rooms feature snappy amenities such as Pop Art pillows, bathrobes and almond cologne, and the hammam, cupola-topped Karma suite and yoga classes get guests catwalk-ready. But even supermodels couldn't resist Fatima's lamb melting into roast quince and other seasonal treats, served atop the tallest roof terrace around.

RIAD AL MASSARAH $$$
☎ 0524 383206; www.riadalmassarah .com; 26 Derb Jedid; ✂ 🛜 ⬛
The ultimate feel-good hideaway: British-French owners Michel and Michael redesigned this ancient riad to maximise comfort and sunlight, and minimise electrical and water use and eco-impact. Offers top-notch hammam, massages, cooking lessons, and ecofriendly excursions – all while donating to a Marrakesh shelter for street children and providing full benefits to a staff of five.

RIAD ALTAÏR $$
☎ 0524 385254; www.riadaltair.com; 21 Derb Zaouia, off Rue Fatima Zohra; 🅿 ✂ 🛜 ⬛ ⚕
Star-crossed lovers find happy endings at Altaïr, named for the eagle constellation that seems within reach from the panoramic two-storey terrace. Altaïr is a natural charmer, with sand-worn cedar doors and exposed brick archways opening onto six airy, cushy, effortlessly elegant rooms. Bustling Bab Doukkala souq is around the corner, but nesting instincts prevail here.

RIAD EL-SAGAYA $
☎ 0524 380353; www.riad-elsagaya .com; 150 Arset Ihiri; ✂ ⬛ ⚕
London law-firm escapee Annabella and her husband Youssef offer laid-back hospi-

tality and 10 cheerful, sunset-hued guestrooms with *tadelakt* bathrooms. Staff organise babysitting plus loads of activities, from *tadelakt* workshops with a master artisan and henna tattooing lessons to accompanied public hammam trips and ecofriendly mountain treks.

RIAD JULIA
$

☎ 0524 376022; www.riadjulia.com; 14 Derb Halfaoui; ✖ 🍴 👶
How clever – each room highlights a Marrakesh handicraft, from mother-of-pearl inlay to chip-carved cedar wood. Five of the seven rooms have air conditioning, and all are well-kept and comfy, including bathrobes and soft Berber wedding blankets with coin fringes for good luck (wink, wink). English-speaking Ziad arranges excursions, henna tattooing and dinners under the Berber roof tent. Babysitting available.

RIAD KNIZA
$$$

☎ 0524 376942; www.riadkniza.com; 34 Derb L'Hotel; ✖ 🖥 🛜 🍴 👶
Gregarious grandeur in an 18th-century mansion restored by antiques aficionado Mohammed Bouskri. In cushy salons and on sunny patios, people mingle easily, staff take the time to chat, and drinks are constantly refreshed. Learn to make signature lamb and chicken dishes, soak in the new

> ## TOP FIVE FOR STYLE
> > Riad Enija (p128)
> > Riad Magellan (p121)
> > Noir d'Ivoire (p125)
> > Tchaikana (p129)
> > Riad Altaïr (p126)

spa or be whisked off to Palmeraie camel or horseback rides by English-speaking chauffeurs. For every booking, Dh50 is donated to charities. Babysitting is available.

RIAD SAHARA NOUR
$$

☎ 0524 376570; www.riadsaharanour-marrakech.com; 118 Derb Dekkak
Learn something new every day at this artistically inclined guesthouse, where you can roll out of bed and into a class on Middle Eastern dance or Moroccan calligraphy. Classes are open to nonguests and subject to separate booking, so reserve early and ask about English-speaking instructors.

CENTRAL SOUQS & DERB DEBACHI

DAR HANANE
$$

☎ 0524 377737; www.dar-hanane.com; 9 Derb Lalla Azzouna; ✖ 🖥 🛜 👶
Lolling comes easily with high-thread-count linens, iPod docking stations and soothing, minimalist decor. The loft living room features

RIADS

BEYOND LOOKS: CHOOSING YOUR RIAD

On the web you'll find hundreds of riads in Marrakesh that appear picture-perfect, candlelit and strewn with rose petals. But some lovely riads aren't licensed, which means you have no guarantees of upkeep, hygiene and decent workplace conditions, where workers get at least the US$0.50/hour minimum wage and time off. Some 200 unlicensed riads were summarily closed by the government in spring 2003, leaving travellers stranded without accommodation in high season.

The licensed riads in this chapter have been selected not on looks alone, but for convenient locations, helpful staff, home-cooked Moroccan meals and must-have Marrakshi experiences such as cooking courses, mountain excursions and hammams. Lonely Planet recommends riads that promote environmentally sustainable practices, fair compensation, time off for employees, cultural exchange and genuine Moroccan hospitality. You can help: give riad feedback at www.lonelyplanet.com/contact.

an honesty bar where you track your Bonassia Cabernet intake (ahem). Chef Aisha's flair for French and Moroccan specialities makes restaurant trips unnecessary, but English-speaking staff organises excursions for the restless.

DAR TAYIB $
☎ 0524 383010; www.riad-dartayib .com; 19 Derb Lalla Azzouna; ✂ ▨
Other riads have glamour, but this place has *baraka* (good vibes). Marrakshi Latifa and French architect husband Vincent bring on the Berber charm, from good-luck-symbol carpets to winking tinwork lamps. The Yasmina room beats love potions with a canopy bed, tub and mood lighting, and clever rooftop hideaways end writer's block. Vincent arranges excursions, and Latifa organises dinners and cooking classes.

RIAD EL BORJ $$
☎ 0524 391223; www.riadelborj.com; 63 Derb Moulay Adbelkader; ✂ ▢ ◉ ▨
This was once Grand-Vizier Madani Glaoui's lookout, and now you too can lord it over the neighbours in the suite with original *zellij*, double-height ceilings and skylit tub. Or try the tower hideaway with the rippled ceiling and book nook. Loaf by the pool in the 'Berber annex', let off steam in the hammam, or take advantage of mountain excursions and babysitting.

RIAD ENIJA $$$
☎ 0524 440926; www.riadenija.com; 9 Derb Mesfioui; ✂ ▢ ▨
Live a charmed existence next door to Rahba Kedima magic sellers at the exquisite Enija. Brushing

up against the 280-year-old architecture are modern design showpieces, rare plants, turtles and supermodels. Drift off on a boat in the Anenome Room or a royal Egyptian barque in the Pourpre Room; awake for brunch in the garden and indulge in facials from the in-house beautician and dips in the new pool. Wi-fi available.

RIYAD EL CADI $$$
☎ 0524 378655; www.riyadelcadi.com; 87 Derb Moulay Abdelkader; ✗ 💻 🔊
A Medina within the Medina, this labyrinth of five riads offers unexpected delights at every turn: lovers' balconies, secret alcoves, a Marrakshi red hammam and glimpses of an outstanding collection of rare Berber textiles. A staff of 15 keeps occupants happy in 12 pristine rooms and suites, ranging from the mod black-and-white double Aleppo to the elegant two-bedroom Douiriya junior suite.

TCHAIKANA $$
☎ 0524 385150; www.tchaikana.com; 25 Derb el Ferrane, Azbest; 🔊
With a Tuareg tent-post bed in one room and a boat suspended from the ceiling in another, Tchaikana has the adventurous spirit of a true Marrakesh caravansari. Travellers plot souq forays over lavish breakfasts hosted by English-speaking Belgian owner Jean-Francois, and return down the winding *derb* at happy hour to compare bargains and plan Sahara eco-adventures.

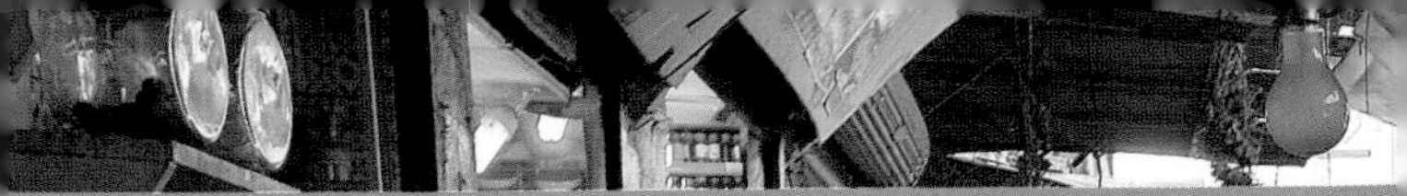

>SNAPSHOTS

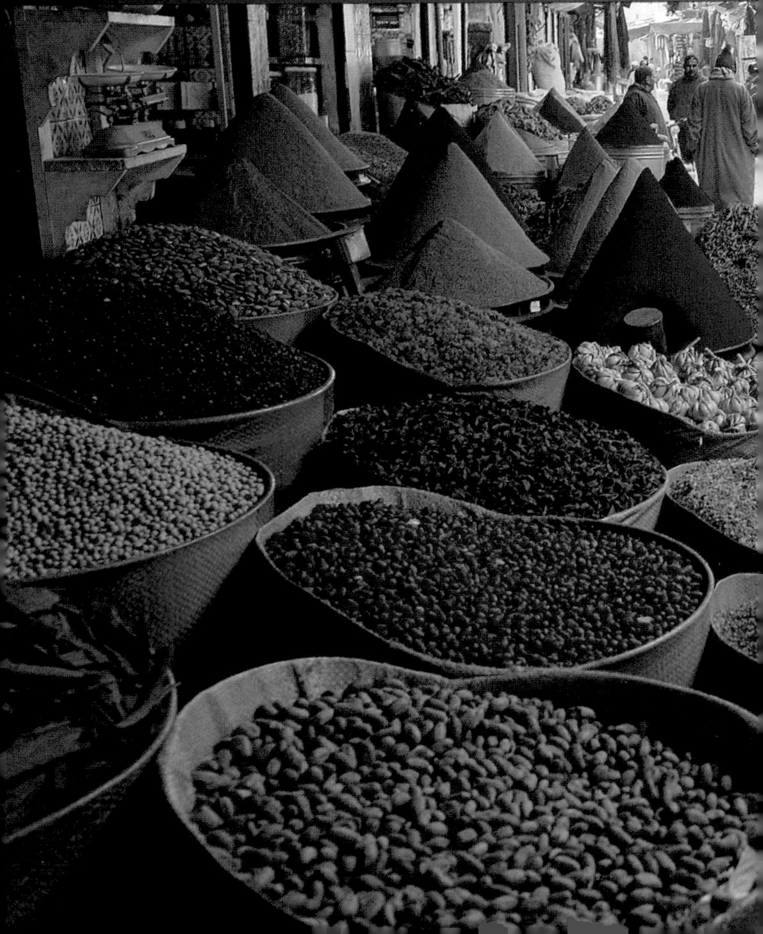

'Dull moment' doesn't translate in Marrakesh, because there are none here – especially if you know where to look. Discover the city's best-kept secrets, and find your own keyhole-shaped niche.

The vibrant colours and stimulating aromas of the souq are the essence of daily life in Marrakesh

SNAPSHOTS

ACCOMMODATION

'Are you happy? Everything's good? How about your family?' What could be the start of a therapy session elsewhere is a greeting in Marrakesh – hospitality has been practised and perfected for a millennium at this trading post. Courtyard fountains are elegantly strewn with rose petals, mint tea is poured from on high without splashing and cosy *bhous* (seating nooks) invite conversation. Riads (courtyard mansions) offer Marrakshi hospitality at its most idyllic; see p117 for listings. For the best riad rates, go for three days or more in low season, or email the riad to ask if you can be accommodated in your price range and on your dates.

The personal attention of a riad can't be matched by a 100-room resort, but Marrakesh's best hotels offer convenience and consistency, and in high season (p120) may be your only choice. The swankiest are in the Hivernage, including historic **Mamounia** (www.mamounia.com). The best value are in downtown Guéliz amid boutiques, galleries and local-favourite restaurants: **Oudaya** (www.oudaya.ma), **Hôtel du Pacha** (☎ 024 431326), **Caspien** (www.lecaspien-hotel.com), **Toulousain** (www.geocities.com/hotel_toulousain) and the pleasant, train-station-handy **Meryem** (www.hotelmeryem-marrakech.com).

When choosing a location in the Medina, follow your bliss. Budget hotels cluster around the Djemaa el-Fna, ranging from cheerfully well travelled to woefully world-weary. Central Mouassine has the most historic homes hidden amid souqs and mosques – bring earplugs to muffle 5am calls to prayer. Palaces and museums cluster in the Riads Zitoun and royal Kasbah, and main streets from the Djemaa el-Fna to the Bahia Palace are lined with artisans. You'll be taking more taxis if you stay in the Kasbah but you'll get more glimpses of authentic Marrakshi neigh-

lonely planet Hotels & Hostels

Need a place to stay? Find and book it at lonelyplanet .com. Over 50 properties are featured for Marrakesh – each personally visited, thoroughly reviewed and happily recommended by a Lonely Planet author. From hostels to high-end hotels, we've hunted out the places that will bring you unique and special experiences. Read independent reviews by authors and other travellers, and get practical information including amenities, maps and photos. Then reserve your room simply and securely via Hotels & Hostels – our online booking service. It's all at lonelyplanet.com/hotels.

bourhood life. Though Derb Debachi is next to bustling Djemaa and Rahba Kedima, its hushed backstreets seem a world apart. Bab Doukkala is convenient to the Nouvelle Ville, and this medieval maze has its own food souqs, boutiques, hammams and upmarket restaurants.

Villas in the Palmeraie let you chill out in a palm oasis. **Les Deux Tours** (www.les-deuxtours.com) is splendid modern-Moroccan and it kicked off the Palmeraie trend; **Dar Ayniwen** (www.dar ayniwen.com) is a family-run eclectic retreat (check out the champagne buckets). Most Palmeraie guesthouses feature pools, hammams, gardens and lounge bars – **Jnane Tamsna** (www .jnanetamsna.com) and **Bled al-Fassia** (www.bledalfassia.com) offer organic cooking courses, while **Riad Bledna** (www.riadbledna.com) offers a range of arts courses including weaving, *tadelakt* (polished plaster), *zellij* (mosaic) and *zellij* patchwork quilting (see boxed text, p66). Environmentally savvy golfers will check into **La Pause** (www.lapause-marrakech.com), an Agafay Desert oasis 30 minutes away with its sod-free, all-terrain course for golf and disc golf.

Last-minute and package deals are listed on Marrakesh's main accommodation websites: www.ilove-marrakech.com, www.maroc-selection .com, www.terremaroc.com and www.riadsmorocco.com. Many riads and villas can be rented by the week: check listings on www.marrakech-riads .net, www.marrakech-medina.com and www.habibihomes.com.

BEST UNDER DH700
> Riad Eden (www.riadeden -marrakech.com)
> Riad Julia (p127; www.riadjulia.com)
> Dar Tayib (p128)
> Riad Nesma (p124)
> Les Jardins de Mouassine (p121)

BEST FOR ROMANCE
> Riad Akka (p123)
> Riyad el Cadi (p129)
> La Sultana (www.lasultana marrakech.com)
> Riad Al Massarah (p126)
> Riad Enija (p128)

BEST OFF THE BEATEN PATH
> Tchaikana (p129)
> Dar Soukaina (p124)
> Maison Mnabha (p122)
> Riad Ifoulki (p123)
> Riad Magellan (p121)

BEST OASIS ESCAPES
> Jnane Tamsna (www.jnane tamsna.com)
> Les Deux Tours (www.les-deux tours.com)
> Dar Ayniwen (www.dar-ayniwen.com)
> Riad Bledna (www.riadbledna.com)
> La Pause (www.lapause -marrakech.com)

FOOD

Even atheists find foodie religion in Marrakesh, where the dishes keep coming until you protest *'Alhamdullilah'*, or 'Praise be to God'. Breakfast on *beghrir*, pancakes with a spongy crumpet texture drizzled with cactus flower honey; lavishly lunch on *mechoui*, slow-roasted almond-stuffed lamb served with cumin, olives and *khoobz* (bread); and after several laps of the souqs, you'll muster appetite for a savoury, seasonal tagine (clay-pot stew) in the Djemaa el-Fna. Few things make Marrakshis happier than to see guests eat with gusto, so go on, do your part for international relations and have dessert. Leave room for *kaab el-ghazal* (crescent-shaped 'gazelle's horn' cookies stuffed with almond paste and laced with orange-flower water) or dessert *bastilla* (layers of flaky pastry with cream and toasted nuts).

In the Nouvelle Ville, you can join Marrakesh's rising middle class for pizza at La Chat Qui Rit (p52) and Catanzara (p51) or barbecue at sidewalk restaurants along Rue ibn Aicha. Fashionable Marrakshis prefer restaurants that do double duty as discos (see p139). Alcohol is now served in many, but not all, restaurants; see individual reviews for details.

For superb home-style cooking, try a riad, where meals are made to order by the in-house *dada* (cook). Adventurous eaters tuck into steaming bowls of snails or sheep's-head stew at thronged stalls in the Djemaa el-Fna (p72) or Ben Youssef Food Stall Qissaria (p87).

For a big night out, Marrakesh has some fantastic Moroccan, Mediterranean and fusion restaurants – but also many tourist-trap 'palace restaurants'. If your footsteps echo, your waiter is sheepishly costumed like Aladdin and there's a stage set up for a laser-light show, don't expect authentic cuisine. Hold out for a proper *diffa* (feast; see p21) at the places recommended below, and a heartfelt *'Alhamdullilah'*.

BEST INVENTIVE MOROCCAN
> Dar Moha (p93)
> Villa Flore (p104)
> Terrasse des Épices (p103)
> Le Foundouk (p88)
> Riad 72 (p94)

BEST TRADITIONAL MOROCCAN
> Al Fassia (p48)
> Souk Kafé (p88)
> La Maison Arabe Restaurant (p94)
> Tobsil (p103)
> Chez Chegrouni (p72)

BEST STREET EATS
> Mechoui Alley (p74)
> Ben Youssef Food Stall Qissaria (p87)
> Plats Haj Boujemaa (p53) and other grill restaurants on Rue ibn Aicha
> Djemaa el-Fna food stalls (p72)
> Samak al Bahria (p54)

BEST BREAKS FROM MOROCCAN
> Azar (p50)
> Mama Tilee (p114)
> Le Chat Qui Rit (p52)
> La Table du Marché (p52)
> Le Grand Café de la Poste (p53)

Top left Meat-lovers' paradise: Mechoui Alley (p74) **Above** Service with a smile: Souq Ablueh (p81)

TRADITIONAL ARTS

When a twinkling lamp or scarlet handbag catches your eye in the souqs, look around and you might find the *maâlem* (master craftsperson) nearby, already at work on another fabulous creation. This is your chance to extend your compliments, see how it's made, maybe even try your hand at a traditional Moroccan craft – just don't be dismayed if you're not a natural. Marrakshi *maâlems* make their handiwork look easy, but it takes years of apprenticeship and skills handed down through generations to master those medieval tools and time-honoured techniques. A *zellij* apprentice can take months to master just one of the 400-plus essential shapes in *zellij* patterns, and mathematicians have only recently begun to understand the variation-within-repetition 'Penrose patterns' found within Islamic mosaic motifs.

Hot spots to watch *maâlems* work wonders are the north end of the souqs and the Ensemble Artisanal (p40). You often get the best deals on handcrafted goods straight from the maker, but really, in a world of mass-produced, machine-made goods, these labour-intensive crafts are a bargain at any price. Back home, you can't exactly nip round to your local *tadelakt* artisan for a silky, hand-buffed teal vase, or the local weaver for a shimmering, red-carpet-ready cactus-fibre evening wrap. Purchases from travellers have helped keep these vital traditions alive, and continue to push Marrakshi *maâlems* to innovate in an extremely competitive artisans' market.

In Marrakesh, traditional craftsmanship is anything but stodgy. Skilled Marrakshi artisans are often hired by European, Japanese and American designers to execute their ideas, and in turn Marrakshi artisans gain exposure to cutting-edge design from around the world. The result is a polyglot Marrakesh modernism with deep, saturated Moroccan hues, mod organic shapes, and spare geometric and Berber motifs. This inspiration has recently emerged in painting and sculpture, which used to be lesser Moroccan art forms but are now major attractions at Nouvelle Ville galleries, along with ultramodern calligraphy. Go on and add your ideas to the artistic mix: courses in crafts and culinary arts are offered at a number of riads.

BEST PLACES TO SEE MAÂLEMS AT WORK
> The souq circuit (p81)
> Ensemble Artisanal (p40)
> Fondouqs (p98)
> Al Kawtar (p99)
> Sidi Ghanem (p47)

BEST CRAFTS YOU WON'T FIND AT HOME
> Carpet weaving: Ensemble Artisanal (p40)
> *Passimenterie* (hand-knotted trims and tassels): Moulay Youssef el Alaoui (p86)
> Stucco (plasterwork): Sidi Ahmad Gabaz Stucco (p86)
> Ceramic presentation tagines: Chez Adil (p100)
> Tyre crafts: Creations Pneumatiques (p112)

BEST 'NOT SO TRADITIONAL' TRADITIONAL ARTS
> Kifkif (p102)
> Galerie Rê (p40)
> Ministero del Gusto (p103)
> Galerie Noir Sur Blanc (p40)
> Michi (p84)

BEST PLACES TO LEARN FROM LOCAL MASTERS
> Dar Attajmil (p120)
> Jnane Tamsna (p64)
> La Maison Arabe (p125)
> Riad Bledna (p66)
> Riad Sahara Nour (p127)

Left Artisan at work at Ensemble Artisanal (p40)

BERBER CULTURE

Before there were kings, spice traders, or even carpet sellers here, central Morocco was home to the Amazigh, or 'free people' of Saharan, Mediterranean and sub-Saharan African origin. The Romans tried to conquer the Amazigh for 250 years. When they couldn't defeat their foes they badmouthed them, dubbing them 'Berbers' or Barbarians.

The Berber Pride movement has recently reclaimed 'Berber' as a unifying term, and Marrakesh proudly claims Berber roots. Tashelhit is the most common Berber language, and it's widely spoken in Marrakesh: road-test Tashelhit greetings (see p101) and earn a warm welcome for your pronunciation troubles. In the Rahba Kedima you'll see Berber remedies for everything from excess nerdiness (walnut root) to marital issues (galanga). The Berber carpets festooning the souqs were traditionally woven by women for wedding trousseaus, so they often feature symbols warding off bad luck (such as unworthy grooms) and promoting domestic bliss.

One thing you can't buy at any price is *baraka*, loosely described as a state of grace. As one Berber herbalist explains, '*Baraka* doesn't grow on trees – it comes from what you do' (see below for *baraka*-enhancing hints). Aficionados claim that when you've got *baraka*, you're more in sync with your surroundings, people pick up your good vibes and life seems sweeter. *Barakallahlekoum* (*baraka* be with you).

BEST PLACES TO EXPERIENCE BERBER CULTURE
> Imlil and other High Atlas villages (p146)
> Marrakesh Festival of Popular Arts (p24)
> Djemaa el-Fna (p10)
> Maison Tiskiwin (p110)
> Dar Taliba (p157)

BEST WAYS TO GET BARAKA
> Donations to Dar Taliba or other Berber village projects (p157)
> Exchanging Berber pleasantries (see p101)
> Buying from local cooperatives (p113)
> Conserving water to help High Atlas subsistence farmers (p156)
> Tipping Gnaoua musicians and storytellers in the Djemaa (p10)

CLUBS & BARS

By day it's all serene palaces and hardworking souqs, but at night Marrakesh will not rest until a good time is had by all – hence the Ibiza-esque hours of most entertainment venues here and the essential mid-afternoon nap. Around 11pm, Marrakshis turn Nouvelle Ville restaurants into impromptu discos, bars into sing-along stages and outdoor cafes into hook-up hot spots. Many bars are still male dominated, but several actively encourage women to attend with free drinks – take advantage now, before they do the maths. From here it's on to Pacha Marrakesh (p60) or Le Théâtro (p59) until dawn, then a hammam and nap poolside in the Palmeraie to dry out until happy hour.

The Marrakesh nightlife scene has a speakeasy feel – and technically, there are still Moroccan laws on the books against extramarital sex, homosexuality and selling alcohol within view of a mosque (ie everywhere, especially in the Medina). But once night falls and the music starts, cocktails flow on discreet Medina terraces and in thumping Guéliz bars, and glances are traded across crowded Hivernage dance floors. Mind you, certain come-hither looks in almost any Marrakesh watering hole – especially the high-end ones – are strictly professional. At the risk of stating the obvious, steer clear of paid company, so the only thing you'll have to regret tomorrow is that fourth Moroccan mint mojito.

BEST WATERING HOLES
> Azar (p50)
> Churchill Bar (p55)
> Kosybar (p115; pictured above)
> Le Grand Café de la Poste (p53)
> Bab Hotel Pool Lounge & Skybab (p54)

BEST DANCE-FLOOR ACTION
> Pacha Marrakesh (p60)
> Le Comptoir (p55)
> Le Diamant Noir (p59)
> Jad Mahal (p58)
> Le Théâtro (p59)

FAITH & TRADITION

Soaring minarets, intricate calligraphy, mesmerising calls to prayer: much of what thrills visitors to Marrakesh is inspired by faith. As part of their religious practice, many Muslim Marrakshis make time for quiet reflection and prayer, raucous Ramadan celebrations (you're invited; see below) and everyday kindness – zakat (charity) is one of the five pillars of Islam. Marrakesh has seven marabouts (patron saints), but marabouts' zaouias (shrines) are closed to non-Muslims, as are Marrakesh mosques. But one of the most historic religious sites is open to visitors: the spectacular Ali ben Youssef Medersa (p80), a former college of Islamic learning and law.

Marrakesh's crossroads culture draws from interfaith influences. Follow your senses through the streets of Marrakesh and you'll glimpse ancient animist beliefs in Berber homeopathic cures, taste salty, pickled Jewish culinary influences in local cuisine, and hear Gnaoua riffs and rhythms that predate the arrival of Islam in Africa. Wander through Marrakesh's 700-year-old Mellah, or Jewish quarter, and you'll come across Star of David doorknockers, a still-functioning ancient synagogue, and the Miaâra (Jewish Cemetery; p111). Christian and Jewish communities have been established in Morocco for some 1700 years, and they're still active in the Nouvelle Ville at a synagogue, Catholic church and Protestant hall. Multiple religious traditions have inspired an outpouring of creativity in Marrakesh, and the city's rich traditions of poetry, folk dance, storytelling and street theatre offer roles for one and all.

BEST WAYS TO CELEBRATE RAMADAN

> Party in the streets on Aïd al-Fitr (p164)
> Wake up for the predawn adhan from Koutoubia Minaret (p16)
> Practise zakat: donate to a worthy local cause (p157)
> Avoid eating, drinking and smoking in front of hungry, thirsty, jonesing hosts by day (p30)
> Binge on sweets and harira (lentil soup) after sunset in the souqs (p12)

BEST LOCAL TRADITIONS IN ACTION

> Halqa (street theatre): Djemaa el-Fna (p10)
> Literature and storytelling: Café du Livre (p54)
> Fusion Moroccan cuisine: Dar Moha (p93)
> Berber remedies: Rahba Kedima (p83)
> Folk music: Marrakesh Festival of Popular Arts (p24)

GARDENS

When Yusuf bin Tachfin and his fierce Almoravid warriors swept into a campsite now known as Marrakesh, the first thing they did was start to garden. The Almoravids set up the ingenious *khattara* irrigation system that watered royal gardens and still supports the Palmeraie. Today the gardens nurtured by those combative nature-lovers have become a distinguishing feature of the city, from the grand Menara Gardens (p41) to Jardin Majorelle (p41). There's a garden to suit every style: foodies can dine in Nouvelle Ville garden restaurants (p48), sports fans can play tennis and football in Jardin Harti (p58) and stress cases can unwind in the Palmeraie oasis (p62).

With so many gardens, pools and golf courses taxing the millennium-old *khattara* system and tapping water reserves (see p156), Marrakshi gardeners are getting resourceful with grey-water reuse systems and water-conserving plants. One model garden is at Dar Taliba (p157), the nonprofit Berber girls' school in the High Atlas where students learn to identify and cultivate indigenous herbs. Girls who once had no chance of attending school have gone on to study ethno-botany, and compiled a definitive catalogue of Berber medicinal herbs. For a donation, visitors can tour the garden, enjoy some healing tea and find botanical bliss.

BEST MARRAKESH GARDEN ACTIVITIES
> Check email at Cyberpark (p37)
> Enjoy high tea or highballs at sunset in the historic gardens of the Mamounia Hotel (p60)
> Join a *koura* (football) match at Jardin Harti (p58)
> Dine on garden-fresh organic cuisine at Jnane Tamsna (p64)
> Find fresh gardening ideas at Jardin'Art Garden Festival (p24)

BEST GARDENS FOR...
> Inspiration: Dar Taliba (p157)
> Romance: Menara Gardens (p41)
> Art: Jardin Majorelle (p41)
> Royal sightings: Agdal Gardens (p108)
> Kids: Jardin Harti (p58)

SNAPSHOTS

KIDS

The mutual admiration between kids and Marrakesh is obvious. Kids will gaze in wonderment at fairy-tale souq scenes their parents pretend to take in their stride: potion sellers trading concoctions straight out of *Harry Potter*, old tins being hammered into Aladdin-esque lamps, cupboard-sized shops packed with spangled slippers worthy of Cinderella. Since most Marrakshis dote on kids, yours may emerge from the souqs thoroughly spoiled by all the attention, their pockets bulging with treats and faces smeared with sweets.

There's plenty to stimulate young minds and reward good behaviour after a day of sightseeing. Active imaginations go wild in splendid palaces and kids get a second wind with treats from Dino (p52) or Venezia Ice (p75). Kids used to leashed pets and packaged meats will surely be surprised to see animals wandering about, pulling carts or being sold in markets – and this could be the start of a most educational conversation. When grown-up company becomes tiresome, gardens are usually good for impromptu play dates. For family fun, try camel safaris, pony rides and pools in the Palmeraie (p62).

Marrakesh's facilities aren't always ideal for kids – riads with unattended plunge pools, steep steps and low electrical outlets aren't childproof – and bear in mind that some of your fellow guests in intimate riad quarters may not take kindly to boisterous toddlers. To find the most kid-friendly venues, look for the 🏃 symbol throughout this guide. See individual reviews for babysitting services, and ask about English-speaking services when booking.

BEST TREATS
> Venezia Ice (p75)
> Alrazal (p42)
> ZidZid Kids in Sidi Ghanem (p47)
> Gnaoua Music Shop (p112)
> Café 16 (p50)

BEST HANGOUTS
> Kawkab Jeux (p58)
> Flower Power Café (p57)
> Cyberpark (p37)
> Jardin Harti (p58)

PAMPERING

Radiant skin and relaxed attitudes are far more common than you'd expect this close to the Sahara in the midst of souq traffic – and for that, you can thank the *tebbaya*. A *tebbaya* is the hero of the hammam (traditional Moroccan bathhouse) who performs the essential *gommage*, the exfoliating treatment done with gummy *savon noir* (literally 'black soap'; natural palm soap) and a *kessa* (rough-textured glove).

A hammam might sound decadent, but it's one of the best deals in Marrakesh. Entry and *gommage* cost just Dh30 to Dh50 at a community hammam (expect to pay Dh150-plus at a riad hammam). And you'll leave with a clean conscience, too: once the day's steam gets going, a gorgeous *gommage* uses fewer resources than most showers. At any community hammam, you'll need your own plastic mat, flip-flops, towel and a change of undies – you'll be expected to wear yours so they'll get wet.

You might also opt for *rhassoul*, a mud scalp rub, or a massage with healing oils of argan (for stressed-out skin) or arnica (for sore muscles). Fancy hammams in the Palmeraie and Nouvelle Ville offer speciality treatments including Jacuzzis, facials with local herbs, and four-handed massages with two masseurs plying sore muscles. Women traditionally get henna tattoos to mark celebrations in Marrakesh, and your vacation is surely an occasion to celebrate. But be sure to avoid 'black henna', a mix of synthetic dyes that can cause your skin to blister – go with all-natural (aka 'red' or 'green') henna instead. See p18 for more.

BEST AUTHENTIC HAMMAMS

> Hammam Bab Doukkala (p95)
> Hammam Dar el-Bacha (p95)
> Bain d'Or (p89)
> Les Deux Tours Hammam (p67)
> Ksar Char-Bagh Hammam (p67)

BEST MOROCCAN SPA TREATMENTS

> *Gommage*: Hammam Dar el-Bacha (p95)
> Four-handed massage: Sultana Spa (p116)
> Threading: Maison Arabe (p95)
> Honey scrub: Mamounia Spa & Wellness (p60)
> *Takssila* (stretching): Raid Spa Bahia Salam (p115)

PERFORMING ARTS

All the world may be a stage, but Marrakesh has been stealing the show for 1000 years. *Halqa* (street theatre) performers make you stop and stare at triple flips, gyrating cobras and belly dancers with double-jointed hips. When an act is riveting, an encore is assured by providing generous tips.

Movies are not your average multiplex fare here. You'll see Marrakshis lining up for independent films at Institut Français (p57) and all-male crowds singing along to Bollywood musicals at Cinéma Eden (p77). The crowd goes wild at the Marrakesh International Film Festival (p26) – especially at open-air screenings in the Djemaa el-Fna.

Many restaurants feature live music and belly dancing nightly. Technically, belly dancing is an Ottoman tradition, but in Djemaa el-Fna they aren't hung up on such technicalities – these dancers are cross-dressing men.

The city's cultural institutions also put on quite a show. Big-name acts perform at Théâtre Royal (p61), Institut Français (p57) and Badi Palace (p108). Moroccan stars take to the streets at the Marrakesh Festival of Popular Arts (p24) and you can also discover local acts on CDs at Kifkif (p102) and Le Comptoir (p55).

BEST LIVE PERFORMANCES
> Djemaa el-Fna (p70)
> Marrakesh Festival of Popular Arts (p25)
> Théâtre Royal (p61)
> Institut Français (p57)
> Openings at Dar Chérifa (p98)

BEST FOR MUSIC
> Djemaa el-Fna (p70)
> Essaouira Gnaoua Music Festival (p24)
> Théâtre Royal (p61)
> MadJazz (p24)
> Essaouira Alizés (Trade Winds) Classical Music Festival (p24)

BEST VENUES FOR DANCE
> Djemaa el-Fna (p70)
> Riad Sahara Nour (p127)
> Institut Français (p57)
> Théâtre Royal (p61)
> Marrakesh Festival of Popular Arts (p24)

BEST MOVIE MAGIC
> Marrakesh International Film Festival (p26)
> Cinéma Colisée (p57)
> The perfume 'Festival' at Les Parfums du Soleil (p44)
> Bollywood singalongs at Cinéma Eden (p77)
> Institut Français (p57)

SHOPPING

Who knew shopping could be so enlightening? You can glimpse a *maâlem's* mosaic techniques, learn Berber sunburn remedies from apothecaries and get the ceremonial mint-tea treatment in carpet shops. You can probably get that pillowcase made to match your sofa or a suit tailored to fit, and artisans will proudly show you how it's done. Factor friendly banter into your shopping time for a warm reception and probably a better price – everything is negotiable in the souqs except obligatory pleasantries. Whether you buy or not, the shopkeeper will remember you tomorrow, and greet you with '*Labes?*' ('Happy?') At these prices, who wouldn't be?

The two barriers to a Marrakshi overhaul of your home decor and wardrobe are cash and shipping. Credit cards and travellers cheques are usually not accepted in the souqs. Some Medina merchants might offer you 'Berber credit', where you pay most of the purchase price and take your purchase, returning with the balance later. Shoppers pressed for time will prefer fixed (though usually higher) prices and credit-card machines in the Nouvelle Ville. It can cost as much as you paid for your carpet to ship it home, so travel with empty suitcases.

Most shops in the souqs open by 10am and stay open until 7pm, only closing on Friday afternoon. Nouvelle Ville stores are open Monday to Saturday by 10am, close from 1.30pm to 3.30pm, then open again until 7pm.

BEST BARGAIN GIFTS

> Essential oil soaps from L'Art du Bain Savonnerie Artisanale (p102)
> Hand-beaten felt flowers from Masroure Abdillah (p102)
> Mini tagines from Mademoiselle Ibtissam's Original Design (p113)
> Tigmi Cooperative coasters from Jamade (p112)
> Jewellery boxes of responsibly sourced thuya wood from Cooperative Artisanale Femmes de Marrakech (p84)

BEST SOUVENIRS THAT AREN'T CARPETS

> Michelin tyre photo-frame from Creations Pneumatiques (p112), featuring your best souq shot
> Flour-sack slippers from Michi (p84)
> Argan massage oil from Assouss Cooperative d'Argane (p99)
> Recycled metal castanets from Gnaoua Music Shop (p112)
> Berber power-symbol tunic from Kasbek/Chez Amal & Tiftif (p113)

SPORT & ADVENTURE

As if laps of the souqs weren't enough of a workout, Marrakesh packs in adventures for the hyperactive. You can find tennis, fellow joggers and stadium football in Jardin Harti (p58), and pick up football games on almost any spare patch of *piste* (hard-packed earth). The Palmeraie offers more sporting options: horseback riding, camel rides, and less frenetic roads for cyclists and serious runners than in town. Swimming, gyms and exercise classes are mostly limited to Nouvelle Ville hotels or Palmeraie guesthouses. Gym junkies can try Canal Forme (p57), a gym-spa open to nonmembers. But in the dry midday heat, most locals leave physical feats of daring to the acrobats in the Djemaa el-Fna.

Great outdoor adventures await just outside Marrakesh in the mountain villages around picturesque Imlil, hidden oases of the High Atlas, and the pre-Saharan desert. While you can't get to Saharan dunes in a weekend from Marrakesh without harrowingly reckless driving over mountain passes, you can get a breathtaking desert experience in an afternoon in the Agafay Desert, 40km from Marrakesh. In this desert, La Pause (p133) offers overnight stays, organic meals and eco-friendly all-terrain golf, and **Inside Morocco Tours** (www.insidemoroccotours.com) hosts picnics in a Berber ghost town. Ask eco-travel guide Mohamed Nour about combining this picnic with an overnight stay in Imlil and his 'Secret Valleys Tour', visiting Berber villages that cling to cliffs in High Atlas oases.

BEST LOCAL SPORTS

> All-terrain golf and disc golf in the desert at La Pause (www.lapause -marrakech.com)
> *Koura* in Jardin Harti (p58)
> Running the Marathon of Marrakesh (p24)
> Horseback, camel and bike riding in the Palmeraie (p64 and p66)
> Bargaining in the souqs (p12)

BEST QUICK ADVENTURES

> High Atlas treks near Imlil (www .insidemoroccotours.com)
> Ghost-town picnics in the Comune de Agafay Desert (www.insidemo roccotours.com)
> Essaouira beach break by bus (p160)
> Diversity Excursions to the Saharan oasis of Skoura (www.diversity -excursions.co.uk)
> *Calèche* ride around the ramparts (p71) or Palmeraie (p64 and p66)

>BACKGROUND

The souqs: always entertaining

BACKGROUND

HISTORY

Youssef ben Tachfine, the brilliant Almoravid strategist who conquered Spain, saw potential in this trading post strategically located between the desert, mountains and the sea, and built ramparts around it in 1062. His son Ali ben Youssef's dedication to prayer, fasting and construction projects did wonders for the city's architecture and irrigation systems – but not so much for the Almoravids' military standing against the Almohads, a rival Berber tribe. The Almohads' founder was tossed out of Mecca for berating pilgrims who weren't praying hard enough. These pious pillagers swept into town in 1147, razing the first Koutoubia Mosque, which was mis-aligned with Mecca, but mysteriously leaving the Koubba Ba'adiyn intact.

Under Almohad Yacoub el-Mansour (the Victorious), Marrakesh became an imperial capital with a fortified Kasbah, new mosques (the rebuilt Kou-toubia Mosque and the Kasbah Mosque), glorious gardens (including the Menara and Agdal Gardens), *qissarias* (covered markets) and a triumphal gate (Bab Agnaou) – only to lose it all to the Merenids, who preferred Meknès and Fez. After two centuries as a capital, Marrakesh was reduced to its humble origins as a trading outpost. By the time the Saadians took control in the early 16th century, the city was decimated by famine.

SWEET & SOUR

Sugar made life sweet again when the Saadians made Marrakesh the focal point of their lucrative sugar trade route. Sultan Moulay Abdallah created a Jewish quarter (the Mellah) outside the Kasbah in 1558 and a trading centre for Christians – generous gifts that these communities repaid many times over in taxes. With the proceeds, the Sultan rebuilt the Almoravid Ali ben Youssef Mosque and Merenid Medersa. His succes-sor, Ahmed el-Mansour Eddahbi (the Victorious and Golden), had more worldly ambitions, paving the Badi Palace with gold and precious stones, and taking opulence to the grave with the sumptuous Saadian Tombs.

But as any storyteller in the Djemaa el-Fna might've predicted, the good life wouldn't last for Marrakesh. The city lapsed into lawlessness until the Arab Alawites brought long-term stability (the current king is descended from this dynasty). But Marrakshis might have preferred anarchy to early Alawite leader Moulay Ismail, whose idea of fun was performing amateur dentistry on anyone who irked him. Lucky for Marrakshis fond of their teeth, Moulay Ismail preferred docile Meknès to unruly Marrakesh, and moved his headquarters there – though not before looting the Badi Palace.

PALACES & PIE

Marrakesh entered its Wild West period, when big guns vied for control over local trades in goods and slaves. Those who prevailed built extravagant riads, but the Medina walls were left to crumble, once-grand gardens filled with garbage and much of the population lived hand to mouth in crowded *fondouqs* (rooming houses). In the 19th century Sultan Moulay Hassan built the extravagant Bahia Palace, bankrolled by increasingly disgruntled Marrakshi taxpayers.

Meanwhile, European colonial powers began breaking off pieces of North Africa like hunks of tasty *bastilla* (pigeon pie). Sultan Moulay Abdelaziz tried to ally with the British, but Britain abandoned him. Abdelaziz then had to contend with the French, the Spanish and his own people, who'd had enough of paying taxes to bankroll his expensive European tastes.

A local Berber warlord named Thami el-Glaoui proved much more adept at bartering with the French and repressing his own people. In 1912 the French résident-général anointed Thami el-Glaoui pasha of Marrakesh with impunity to do as he wished, which included extorting protection money, executing rivals, kidnapping women and children who struck his fancy, and playing golf with Ike Eisenhower and Winston Churchill. Legend has it that before the pasha left Marrakesh to attend Queen Elizabeth II's coronation, a fresh display of human heads decorated his palace to dissuade nationalists agitating for independence. The heads didn't work, nor did exiling nationalist sympathiser King Mohammed V. The pasha came to a bitter end in 1956, wracked with cancer and begging the King's forgiveness.

IMPERIAL AGAIN

The new constitutional monarchy was established by Mohammed V and taken over in 1961 by his controversial son Hassan II. In 1975 Hassan II ordered the Green March, a military-escorted contingent of 300,000 Moroccan citizens from Marrakesh into Western Sahara to establish Morocco's claim on the former Spanish colony (and its phosphate and oil resources), which sparked an ongoing conflict. With a growing gap between rich and poor, and a mounting tax bill to cover military debt, Hassan II suppressed trade unionists, women's rights activists, Islamists, journalists, Berbers and the working poor – a cross-section of Moroccan society – which led to mass protests in 1981. Hundreds were killed, 1000 wounded, and an estimated 5000 protesters arrested in a nationwide *laraf* (roundup).

At the urging of Morocco's human rights advocates, the extreme measures of Hassan II's black years have been curbed by Mohammed VI. Today Morocco has one of the cleaner recent human rights records in the Middle East and Africa, with an Equity and Reconciliation Commission to investigate political prisoners' mistreatment. Since municipal and parliamentary elections were introduced in 2007, women have been elected to offices nationwide – including lawyer Fatima Zahra Mansouri, elected mayor of Marrakesh in 2009 at age 33. Public demand for greater democratic participation, poverty alleviation and press freedoms has outpaced government liberalisation efforts, prompting nationwide demonstrations in 2011 demanding government reforms. But while Rabat takes two steps forward, one step back, Marrakesh hurtles forward as the capital of Morocco's tourism industry, with a cosmopolitan outlook that's true to its history and promising for its future.

LIFE AS A MARRAKSHI

For a millennia-old civilization, Marrakesh sure looks young for its age. There's a reason for this, beyond all those rejuvenating hammams: over

MARRAKSHI SOCIAL GRACES

> Do accept mint tea whenever it's offered, even if you just take a sip.
> Do avoid clingy or revealing clothes, whether you're a man or a woman. Many Marrakshis wear skimpy clothes, especially to clubs. But if you do, you'll be avoided by elderly Marrakshis, who believe proper attire signifies respect for your hosts and their customs – and you'll be missing out on excellent company.
> Do greet Marrakshis you've met warmly: shake hands, then touch your heart with your right hand. Women may kiss one another on the cheek three times, and men clasp one another's hands for a long, long time. Men and women might exchange a handshake and air-kiss if they're good friends.
> Don't drink alcohol in public areas; if there's a mosque nearby (and there usually is), it's considered insensitive.
> Don't smooch in public. Even hand-holding between men and women makes many locals uncomfortable – though it's common between men who are friends, and among women as well.
> Don't take pictures without asking permission first. Many Muslims believe that humans are created in God's image, and attempting to capture God's reflection is hubris. Other objections are strictly practical, including Marrakshi artisans concerned others may copy their designs.

half Morocco's population is under 20 years old. Primary education to the age of 14 is now required and model initiatives around Marrakesh are working hard to reduce female illiteracy rates as high as 60% – Moroccan girls account for almost 66% of the half a million Moroccan children under the age of 15 who work instead of getting an education. To help keep kids in school, only make purchases from adults; don't give kids handouts – it teaches them to beg and shames their parents, so consider charities listed in the boxed text (p157) instead; and, at the risk of sounding like your own grandma, urge kids to study hard.

While Moroccan society revolves around the family, young Moroccans are increasingly leaving home and delaying marriage to pursue careers in Marrakesh. Not that it's always easy to find jobs: unemployment for Moroccans aged 25 to 44 years approaches 20%. Moroccans living in France, Germany, Spain and the USA – whose remittances to family back home represent as much as 20% of GDP – are increasingly sponsoring family members to pursue studies and careers abroad. But for go-getters in the booming hospitality sector, Marrakesh offers exceptional opportunities.

AIMING TO PLEASE

Seven days a week, no matter how early you rise in the morning, there's already someone in the souqs (covered market streets) to greet you in several languages: 'Hello, come in, you're welcome in Marrakesh'. This isn't just lip service – historically Marrakesh is a crossroads culture, where the dominant Berber population mingled with Arabs and Gnaoua (freed slaves from sub-Saharan Africa). The city's now-small Christian and Jewish populations are almost as old as the city itself, and Europeans have been a constant presence for more than a century. But though cosmopolitan locals won't be surprised to see you, they'll certainly be pleased: your visit duly honours their culture and their city, and your contributions go a long way in an economy where the minimum hourly wage is Dh3.5.

While you're in town, you'll encounter some of the many European, American and even a few Kiwi expatriates running riads – and incurring a certain amount of resentment for buying up prime Medina real estate, inflating local prices and not paying their fair share of taxes. In turn, some expats accuse locals of narrow-mindedness, so be prepared to take generalisations you hear on either side with a hefty grain of Essaouira sea salt. But cultural differences are not insurmountable in Marrakesh – witness the many intercultural couples you'll meet running riads, restaurants and other businesses.

MAKE MERRY & BE BAHJA

It's not all work and no play for Marrakshis, known across Morocco as the *bahja* (joyous ones). Marrakshis are generous with their time and extend courtesies that might seem to you like impositions, from walking you to your next destination so you don't get lost to inviting you home for tea or lunch. Most nights out are group outings with family or friends, but you'll witness dates in progress in gardens and quiet upper terraces of cafes – and plenty of smoochy faces made via webcam in internet cafes. Among the regular Marrakesh cybercafe crowds of instant messagers, bloggers and internet daters are plenty of Moroccan women, who now account for 30% of all Arab women on the internet. Marrakesh's literati are hardly stuffy, and a good time is had by all at literary cafe and Nouvelle Ville gallery openings. But when Marrakshis take over the streets for festivals, open-air movie screenings and nightly performances in the Djemaa el-Fna, everyone becomes *bahja* (joyous).

ARTS & ARCHITECTURE

Arts aren't a specialised, lofty pursuit here; they're the bright thread that runs through the fabric of Marrakshi life. To track the latest Moroccan cultural developments, check out the Morocco page of the award-

WOMEN IN MARRAKESH

Marrakesh is becoming a destination of choice among women travellers, and it's a comparatively safer place to visit solo than London or New York. What with the plain-clothes police, staff at your riad or hotel, and locals you befriend, someone is always keeping an eye out for you. Marrakshi men are often more respectful than the blokes back home; it may be off-putting to be called 'gazelle', but it's fairly innocuous. Unwanted interactions are easy to end: just walk away. Souq shopkeepers may occasionally tap your shoulder, but otherwise you shouldn't be touched by anyone you don't know. If you ever do feel threatened or harassed, just shout '*Aib!*' (shame). This will get the attention of anyone within earshot, and the provocateur will very likely run away.

Follow the etiquette guidelines (see the boxed text, p150) and you'll soon be at ease among Marrakshi women and men alike. This is a privilege male travellers do not often enjoy, since male-female interactions are still stilted by social convention. Women visitors may meet Marrakshiyyas (Marrakesh women) eager to chat, compare life experiences and exchange ideas about world events. Marrakshiyyas are having their say and taking charge as never before, and you can show your support by visiting Marrakshiyya-run businesses such as Al Fassia (p48) and women's cooperatives (see the boxed text, p113).

LANDMARK SPOTTING
Head to a Medina riad or restaurant rooftop and see if you can spot these local architectural landmarks:

Fondouqs Medieval courtyard compounds that house artisans' workshops downstairs, and travellers, traders and workers upstairs.

Riads Mudbrick courtyard mansions, traditionally centred around a garden with a fountain.

Zaouias *Marabout* (saint) shrines closed to non-Muslims; you'll notice their green-tiled roofs pointing heavenward in the northern Medina.

Hammams Domed public bathhouses let off steam through star-shaped vents, traditionally lined with *tadelakt* (polished plaster).

Fountains Local water sources supplied by ingenious underground irrigation systems sustained Marrakesh through years-long medieval sieges.

winning European-based www.babelmed.net, which features articles on new books, films, travelling art shows, and UN reports in French and English.

ARCHITECTURE
Marrakshi mudbrick architecture may be low to the ground, but it's a monumental achievement. Metre-thick walls absorb heat to keep buildings cool in summer and warm in winter – and building materials don't get much more green than local mud mixed with straw for strength. Buildings more than one storey tall are reinforced with cedar posts and capped with rooftop terraces, where neighbours catch breezes and local gossip in the evenings.

LITERATURE
Watch the storytellers, singers and scribes in the Djemaa el-Fna, and you'll understand how Morocco's literary tradition has remained so vital and irrepressible. William S Burroughs, Paul Bowles and other Beat Generation authors were inspired by the city's storytelling traditions – but Marrakesh also looms large in the Moroccan literary imagination, notably in Marrakshi Mahi Binebine's harrowing 2003 novel *Welcome to Paradise* and Moroccan author Tahar ben Jelloun's Prix Goncourt–winning novel *The Sand Child*. Sociologist Fatima Mernissi, Moroccan feminist and author of the memoir *Dreams of Trespass: Tales of a Harem Girlhood*, memorably describes Marrakesh as 'the city where black and

white legends crossed, languages mingled and religions clashed with the immutable silence of the dancing sands'. So may it be again: despite recent press censorship, poetry readings, literary cafes, book clubs and small publishers are springing up in Marrakesh.

MUSIC

Loud, heartfelt and irresistibly funky Gnaoua music vies for listeners' attention with subtle, Berber-inflected Andalucian classical music, but both reward close listening. Classical musicians strum chords from lutes and ouds that resonate as though they're being played on your heartstrings instead. At times the music speeds up like a racing heartbeat, only to subside to a single note that follows you all the way home. Gnaoua musicians thrum out catchy, bluesy tunes on handmade instruments, including metal castanets, *ribabs* (three-stringed banjos) and plenty of *deffs* (hand-held drums), working themselves and their audience into a joyous trance. The tradition was started in Marrakesh and Essaouira as a ritual of deliverance from slavery that sets spirits free. Lately the big names on the Marrakesh music scene are women's, namely the all-women group B'net Marrakech, and the bold Najat Aatabou, who's the Berber Bob Dylan with her poetic protest songs.

CRAFTS

Marrakshi applied arts and architecture have left viewers agog for centuries, but the recent rage for riad decor has created a visual bonanza in the following art forms.

Carpets and textiles – anything that isn't nailed down in Morocco is likely to be woven, sewn or embroidered, and even then it might be upholstered. Moroccan women are the under-recognised *maâlems* (expert craftspeople) of Moroccan textiles: check out Berber carpets and evening wraps made of *sabra* (cactus silk).

Ceramics – Marrakesh doesn't have much of a ceramics tradition, but has proved a quick study with monochrome Berber-style ceramics, which emphasise striking forms over elaborate decoration.

Woodwork – riad doors and palace ceilings are traditionally made of cedar, and orangewood makes fragrant *harira* (lentil soup) ladles. Knotty, caramel-coloured thuya (conifer indigenous to Morocco) wood is at risk of being admired to extinction, so consider buying thuya crafts from artisans' collectives likely to practise responsible collection and reforesting, such as Cooperative Artisanale Femmes de Marrakech (p84).

THE FINE PRINT

Calligraphy is one of Marrakesh's most cherished art forms and if you look closely, you'll notice the same text by different calligraphers has an incredibly different effect. One might take up a whole page with a single word, while another might fold it origami-style into a flower. The slanting cursive script most commonly used for the Quran is Naskh; cursive letters ingeniously interlaced to form a shape or dense design are hallmarks of the Thuluth style; and high-impact graphic lettering is the Kufic style from Iraq that comes knotted, foliate (vine-like) or square. Check out Galerie Noir Sur Blanc (p40) for abstract modern styles and invent your own style at calligraphy workshops at Dar Bellarj (p80).

Metalwork – pierced brass lamps, iron lanterns and votive candle-holders of recycled sardine tins create instant atmosphere. Any proper Moroccan tea ceremony requires just the right props: gleaming brass teapots and tea trays, engraved and highly polished to reflect well on hosts.

Zellij – puzzle-work mosaic takes decades to perfect, but look out Fez: thanks to the riad decor craze, Marrakshi *maâlems* have more opportunity to hone their craft than Fassi masters.

CONTEMPORARY ART

Marrakesh's art scene has exploded in the past five years, launching Morocco's first biennale, first visual arts school, and first international art fair (p25). Local galleries once catered to tourist demands for kitschy blue-veiled Tuareg figurines and Delacroix-derivative harem painting, but now Nouvelle Ville galleries (p40–1) are taking more risks with cutting-edge calligraphy (see the boxed text, above), installations and paintings. The new 'Marrakesh School' artists combine social commentary, elemental forms, and organic, traditional materials (mud, henna, wax, goatskin).

GOVERNMENT & POLITICS

Marrakshis are known for being outspoken and you'll hear lively political debates in the souqs. The famed 'Berber bluntness' can be refreshing or challenging, depending on which side of the argument you're on, but Marrakshis are consistently generous about differentiating between people and politics. One of the first questions you'll be asked is 'Where are you from?' Whether your answer is Britain, the USA, Afghanistan or Zanzibar, the response is always the same: 'You are welcome in Marrakesh'.

The talk in Marrakesh is well ahead of the political curve in Rabat. Marrakesh's municipal council remains subject to Rabat's control, and draconian government repression of dissent has been criticised by Amnesty International. Marrakshis are known for irreverent humour, but the King is not amused: in 2007, Mohammed VI banned the popular Moroccan publication *Nichane* for a cover article called 'Jokes: How Moroccans Laugh at Religion, Sex and Politics', and an issue of the Moroccan weekly *TelQuel* was pulped for 'failing to respect' the King. But crackdowns haven't stopped Marrakshis from debating politics online, demonstrating in the streets for reforms, or wisecracking in the souqs.

ENVIRONMENT

Many of Morocco's 40,000 wildlife species thrive in the oasis ecosystem of Marrakesh – but there is trouble in paradise. Due to the demands of city dwellers and tourist complexes, 37% of the villages around Marrakesh now lack a reliable source of potable water. Environmentalist Mohammed el Faïz points out the irony that the ultimate garden city – 'the rose amid the palms' – has become both victim and perpetrator of what he calls 'patrimonial vandalism', with lush new real-estate developments demanding ever more water from High Atlas subsistence farmers. According to the Centre for Environmental Systems Research, Morocco ranks in the top 25 nations under the most severe water stress, above the Sudan and Mexico.

GO EASY ON THE ENVIRONMENT

Here's how you can make your holiday low-stress for both you and Marrakesh's delicate desert environment:

Reduce your 'wet footprint' Ask hotel/riad staff to change your linens weekly instead of daily, stay at places with small plunge pools instead of Olympic ones, and enjoy a steamy public hammam instead of a long shower.

Improve your golf game with all-terrain golfing La Pause (p133) offers a rare opportunity to golf as nature intended, on a spectacular turfless course in the Agafay Desert. Marrakesh can't spare the water for the four turf golf courses it already has, let alone two more in the works – consider donating 'green fees' instead to local Berber village projects (see boxed text, opposite).

Venture off the grid Sleep under the stars on gridskipping trips with **Diversity Excursions** (www.diversity-excursions.co.uk), **Mountain Voyages** (www.mountain-voyage.com) or **Inside Morocco Tours** (www.insidemoroccotours.com).

GIVE IT UP FOR MARRAKESH: FOUR WORTHY CAUSES

Atfalouna (www.atfalouna-marrakech.com; � 5-7pm Mon-Thu & Sat) Provides shelter, meals, education and futures to 320 Marrakesh homeless children. Visits possible with two-day notice and Dh400–800 sliding-scale donation.

Education for All (www.efamorocco.org) Builds school dormitories enabling girls to attend school; visitors can volunteer onsite or attend fundraising bike rides.

Reporters without Borders (www.rsf.org) Supports Moroccan journalists facing harassment and jail for publishing articles questioning official policies.

Dar Taliba (☎ 0524 482690; www.globaldiversity.org.uk/north-africa-community-and-conservation; El Hanchane; � Mon-Thu & Sat 3-5pm) Ground-breaking girls' school and botanical garden educating rural girls and keeping Berber botanical knowledge alive. Visits are possible by prior arrangement with a Dh250–500 sliding-scale donation.

FURTHER READING

Hope and Other Dangerous Pursuits is Laila Lalami's celebrated novel about the dreams and fateful decisions of Moroccan immigrants.

Esther Freud's *Hideous Kinky* is a childhood memoir of a magical, haunting two-year pit stop in 1960s Marrakesh along the Hippie Trail.

In *The Polymath*, 2009 Naguib Mahfouz Prize–winner Bensalem Himmich recounts 14th-century scholar Ibn Khuldun's travels and attempts to reason with generals.

Lords of the Atlas, by English historian Gavin Maxwell, tells the true story of the vertiginous rise and prayers-answered fall of the notorious Thami el-Glaoui clan.

The Sand Child is the prize-winning novel about a girl raised as a boy by her father in Marrakesh by Fez-born author and psychotherapist Tahar ben Jelloun.

Welcome to Paradise is Marrakshi Mahi Binebine's breakthrough novel about a smuggler and an accidental fellowship of would-be Moroccan emigrants.

The World's Embrace: Selected Poems is a collection of poems by Abdellatif Laâbi, founder of *Anfas/Souffles* (Breaths), the free-form, free-thinking poetry magazine that landed Laâbi eight years in prison for 'crimes of opinion'. Government censorship notwithstanding, the complete French text of *Anfas/Souffles* is available online at http://clicnet.swarthmore.edu/souffles/sommaire.html.

TOP FIVE MOROCCO BLOGS

> http://lailalalami.com/blog – author Laila Lalami's blog tracks the latest developments in Moroccan and Middle Eastern literature, art and culture.
> www.globalvoicesonline.org/-/world/middle-east-north-africa/morocco – Global Voices Morocco provides a roundup of Moroccan opinion online.
> http://almiraatblog.wordpress.com – blogger Hisham Almiraat offers frank talk about Moroccan democracy, plus critical perspectives on international politics.
> http://gvnet.com/streetchildren/Morocco.htm – keeps tabs on the welfare of Morocco's street children and what you can do to help.
> www.talkmorocco.net – an open forum to discuss Moroccan social issues, democratic reforms, gender roles and popular culture.

FILMS

To find out what Moroccan movies are showing next, check out the program for Morocco's privately run culture channel at www.2M.tv. Look also for the following films in video stores and film festivals near you.

The Man Who Knew Too Much is Hitchcock's 1956 suspense classic about holidaymakers in Morocco accidentally foiling an assassination plot. Hitch plays up Marrakesh's mystique for maximum drama.

Farida ben Lyzaid's 1989 film *A Door to the Sky* tells the story of an émigré's return to Morocco, and her delicate balancing act between activism and tradition.

Bernardo Bertolucci's Golden Globe–winning 1990 epic *The Sheltering Sky* is based on Paul Bowles' breakthrough novel. The film co-stars John Malkovich and Debra Winger as hedonist-protagonists, and southern Morocco as itself.

Hakim Belabbes' 2009 documentary *Ashlaa* (In Pieces) collages 10 years of the director's home-movies into a compelling Moroccan family portrait.

Morocco's 2010 Best Foreign Film Oscar contender was Nour-Eddine Lakhmari's *Casanegra*, about Casablanca youth who live by their wits and confront the White City's darker side.

Jilali Ferhati's 2004 film *Mémoires en Détention* (Memories in Detention) is about an ex-con's efforts to track down relatives of an inmate who lost his memory during his long detention.

Franco-Moroccan director Leila Marrakchi was awarded 'Un Certain Regard' at the 2005 Cannes Film Festival for her first feature *Marock*, about a Muslim girl and Jewish boy who fall in love.

DIRECTORY
TRANSPORT
ARRIVAL & DEPARTURE
AIR

The main point of arrival and departure is **Menara airport** (☎ 0524 447865), a 6km ride southwest of the Medina and Guéliz. *Petits taxis* (local taxis) cost Dh70 by day or Dh100 at night; an airport transfer arranged through your riad (guesthouse) or hotel will cost between Dh150 and Dh200. Airport transfers to/from the Palmeraie cost Dh200.

If this is your first time at the hotel or riad in the Medina, arrange an airport transfer to deliver you to your destination so you don't get lost. Go with

the airport-transfer option to the Palmeraie, as many taxi drivers are unfamiliar with Palmeraie roads. Hotels in Guéliz are easy to access by *petit taxi*.

Low-cost airlines are a benefit to travellers, but a burden on the environment and Marrakesh's air quality; to travel with a cleaner conscience, consider a carbon-offset program (see p161) and a donation to a local nonprofit (p157).

Airport Information
Flight information (☎ 0524 447865)
Information desk (🕑 8am-6pm)
Royal Air Maroc (Map p38, D3; ☎ 0524 436205; www.royalairmaroc.com; 197 Ave Mohammed V, Guéliz; 🕑 8.30am-12.30pm & 2.30-7pm)

Transport Times

	Djemaa el-Fna	Bab Laksour/ Mouassine	Rue de la Liberté	Bahia Palace	Kasbah/ Saadian Tombs	Jardin Majorelle
Djemaa el-Fna	n/a	walk 10min	taxi 5min	walk 15min	walk 20min	taxi 15min
Bab Laksour/ Mouassine	walk 10min	n/a	taxi 5min	taxi 5min	taxi 5min	taxi 10min
Rue de la Liberté	taxi 5min	taxi 5min	n/a	taxi 10min	taxi 10min	taxi 5min
Bahia Palace	walk 15min	taxi 5min	taxi 10min	n/a	walk 5min	taxi 15min
Kasbah/ Saadian Tombs	walk 20min	taxi 5min	taxi 10min	walk 5min	n/a	taxi 20min
Jardin Majorelle	taxi 15min	taxi 10min	taxi 5min	taxi 15min	taxi 20min	n/a

TRAIN

Trains run by the **Office National des Chemins de Fer** (ONCF; ☎ 0524 447768) are convenient and inexpensive. Bookings to Casablanca and beyond can be made at the **main train station** (Map p38, B4; cnr Ave Hassan II & Ave Mohammed VI) or through your riad or hotel.

BUS

Supratours (Map p39, A5; ☎ 0524 435525; Ave Hassan II) offers cushy air-con buses to/from Essaouira and Agadir; book in person or via your hotel/riad. Book buses to/from Fez, Azilal/Cascades d'Ouzoud, Ouarzazate and other Moroccan cities at the new CTM Gare Routière (Map p39, A6; ☎ 0524 434402; Rue Abu Bakr Seddik; ☺ 6am-10pm) southwest of the train station. Buses arrive and depart here; some also stop at Bab Doukkala.

CUSTOMS & DUTY FREE

You can import the following into Morocco without customs duty: 200 cigarettes, 50 cigars or 400g of tobacco; 1L of spirits and 1L of wine; 5g of perfume; and unlimited amounts of foreign currency (amounts over Dh15,000 must be declared).

LEFT LUGGAGE

The **Supratours bus station** (Map p39, A5; Ave Hassan II; per day Dh10; ☺ 6am-10pm) has a room for checked baggage; take valuables with you.

TRAVEL DOCUMENTS

A current passport is required for entry to Morocco, and should be valid for at least six months from the date of entry. Leave plenty of time when arriving and departing to pass through slow-moving customs lines in Marrakesh Menara Airport.

VISA

No visas are necessary for visits under three months for citizens of the UK, USA, Canada, Australia, New Zealand and most Western European countries. South African visitors must have a valid visa from the Moroccan embassy in Pretoria.

RETURN TICKET

A return ticket is required for travellers to Morocco.

GETTING AROUND

Your feet are the best way to get around the Medina, which is mostly closed to car traffic. Driving in Marrakesh is an extreme sport, with scooters zooming from all sides and roundabouts the meek may never escape from – best to leave the driving to unfazed taxi drivers whenever possible. For day trips, you might rent a bike, car or a motorcycle.

BUS

You can't miss the red double-decker buses of **Marrakech Tour** (adult/child day pass Dh130/65; ⏱ every 60min from designated stops), which do a circuit of major Marrakesh landmarks and allow you to get on and off where you please. Check out the Medina and Guéliz with the 'Marrakesh Monumental' tour, or head to the Palmeraie on the 'Marrakesh Romantique' bus.

Public buses leave for the Nouvelle Ville at seemingly random intervals from Place de la Foucauld and cost Dh3. Key bus lines:

No 1: Medina-Guéliz (along Ave Mohammed V)
Nos 3 & 10: Medina–train station
Nos 11 & 18: Medina–Menara Gardens
Nos 4 & 12: Jardin Majorelle–Medina

TAXI

Petit Taxi

These beige compact taxis charge Dh8 to Dh20 by day for trips within Marrakesh, with a Dh10 surcharge at night. Don't bother haggling if the meter is broken; anywhere in town should cost Dh20 max by day, or Dh30 at night. If your party numbers more than three, you must take a *grand taxi,* which requires negotiation.

Prime spots to catch *petit taxis* in the Medina: Gare Routière in Bab Doukkala; Bab Laksour in Mouassine; Bab er-Rob in the Kasbah; the corner of Rue el-Koutoubia and Ave Mohammed V, opposite Koutoubia Minaret, and Ave Houmman el-Fetouaki, near Rue de Bab Agnaou, in Djemaa el-Fna.

In Nouvelle Ville, you'll find that the train station, the corner of Blvd Mohammed Zerktouni and Ave Mohammed V, Place de la Liberté, Place 16 Novembre, and Rue Echouhada in Hivernage are good taxi pick-up spots.

Grand Taxi

These are fancy Mercedes you'll see near *petit taxi* stops and major

---

CLIMATE CHANGE & TRAVEL

Every form of transport that relies on carbon-based fuel generates CO2, the main cause of human-induced climate change. Modern travel is dependent on aeroplanes, which might use less fuel per kilometre per person than most cars but travel much greater distances. The altitude at which aircraft emit gases (including CO2) and particles also contributes to their climate change impact. Many websites offer 'carbon calculators' that allow people to estimate the carbon emissions generated by their journey and, for those who wish to do so, to offset the impact of the greenhouse gases emitted with contributions to portfolios of climate-friendly initiatives throughout the world. Lonely Planet offsets the carbon footprint of all staff and author travel.

hotels. They have no meters, and cost more than *petits taxis* after much haggling, but they'll take up to six people to out-of-town destinations. You can rent them in exclusivity for Essaouira for about Dh400, the Cascades d'Ouzoud for a little less, and Ourika for between Dh200 and Dh300.

CALÈCHES
These are the horse-drawn green carriages you'll see at Place de la Foucauld next to the Djemaa el-Fna. One-way trips within the Medina cost Dh20; otherwise, state-fixed rates of Dh100 per hour apply. Expect a tour of the ramparts to take 1½ hours, and allow three hours for the Palmeraie. In the Hivernage, *calèches* linger outside major hotels along Ave el-Qadissia and Rue Echouhada.

CAR & MOTORCYCLE RENTALS
Rates for car rentals range from Dh450 (from local agencies) to Dh700-plus (from multinational chains) per day; 4WDs cost Dh700 to Dh1000 with minimal insurance. An extra Dh250 to Dh450 could get you a driver, though English-speaking drivers aren't always available.

Local Agencies
Concorde Car (Map p39, B7; ☎ 0524 431116; 154 Ave Mohammed V)

KAT (Map p39, B7; ☎ 0524 433581; 68 Blvd Mohammed Zerktouni; http://membres.lycos.fr/katcar)

Lhasnaoui Rent (Map p38, F1; ☎ 0524 312415; www.lhasnaouirent.com; cnr Ave Allal el-Fassi & Yacoub el-Mansour)

Multinationals
Avis (www.avis.com) Guéliz (Map p39, B8; ☎ 0524 432525; 137 Ave Mohammed V); airport (☎ 0524 433169)

Budget (www.budget.com) Guéliz (Map p38, C2; ☎ 0524 431180; 80 Blvd Mohammed Zerktouni); Mamounia Hotel (☎ 0524 440720; Bab el-Jedid); airport (☎ 0524 438875)

Europcar (www.europcar.com) Guéliz (Map p39, B7; ☎ 0524 431228; 63 Blvd Mohammed Zerktouni); airport (☎ 0524 437718)

Hertz (www.hertz.com) Guéliz (Map p39, B7; ☎ 0524 439984; 154 Ave Mohammed V); airport (☎ 0524 447230)

PRACTICALITIES
BUSINESS HOURS
Hours during summer and Ramadan may vary, but opening hours are usually:

Banks 8.30am to 4.30pm Monday to Friday, 8.30am to 12.30pm Saturday

Nouvelle Ville 10am to 1pm and 3pm to 7pm Monday to Saturday

Medina most 10am to 7pm (some close Friday afternoon and/or Sunday).

CLIMATE & WHEN TO GO
A New Year or Easter holiday in Marrakesh might sound fun, but everyone else has the same idea. Hotels and riads raise their

prices and flights are booked well in advance. For better rates and service, plan around these holidays.

Weather-wise, the best times to go are spring and autumn, when temperatures are 20°C to 25°C by day and at least 10°C by night, and November to February, when nights are cooler but similar daytime temperatures and light rainfall are possible.

The weather in March and April features sporadic, light rainfall with some sandstorms in April, while June sees dusty siroccos (desert winds) sweep through the city. From mid-June to August temperatures rise into the 30s and occasionally 40s.

ELECTRICITY

Voltage 220V
Frequency 50Hz
Cycle AC
Plugs Two round pins

EMERGENCIES

Crime and hustling is actively prevented by the *brigade touristique* (plain-clothes police officers) and locals keeping an eye on their neighbourhoods.

Main streets are relatively safe to walk along even at night, though be wary in dark alleys and mind your wallet as you would anywhere.

EMERGENCY TELEPHONE NUMBERS

Brigade Touristique (☎ 0524 384601)
Fire (☎ 15)
Police (☎ 19)
Polyclinique du Sud (private hospital; Map p38, B2; ☎ 0524 447999

HEALTH

IMMUNISATIONS

None are strictly necessary for Morocco, although hepatitis vaccinations and a tetanus booster are good safeguards.

PRECAUTIONS

The main complaints visitors have in Marrakesh are stomach upset, dehydration and minor skin irritations, most of which can be avoided. Drink plenty of water to avoid dehydration and bring antidiarrhoeal pills to avoid pasha's revenge. Tap water is potable but can take some getting used to, so go for the bottled stuff. With lavish five-course Moroccan dinners, pace yourself and stick to small portions. Steer clear of food stalls with less-than-fresh oil or ingredients, and avoid juice and snack vendors who rinse and reuse drinking glasses or utensils. Sunblock is a must year-round, and powder prevents heat rashes.

MEDICAL SERVICES

Travel insurance is advisable to cover any medical treatment in

Marrakesh; Morocco does not have reciprocal health-care arrangements with other countries. Basic care is inexpensive and can be found at hotel clinics during the day. Emergency medical care is available 24/7 at the **Polyclinique du Sud** (Map p38, B2; ☎ 0524 447999; cnr Rue de Yougoslavie & Rue ibn Aicha). Patients with serious illnesses should fly home to see their own physicians.

DENTAL SERVICES
Emergency dental care can be found at the Polyclinique du Sud and from English-speaking **Dr Bennani** (Map p39, A7; ☎ 0524 431145; 112 Ave Mohammed V).

PHARMACIES
These are clearly marked with a green cross. In the Djemaa el-Fna there's a **late-night pharmacy** (Map p69, B4; ☎ 0524 390238; 9am-midnight); others take turns as *pharmacies du garde* that open until midnight and on weekends – check listings posted on pharmacy doors and windows. After midnight, medications are available at the Polyclinique du Sud. Pharmacie Koutoubia (p93) offers European homeopathic remedies as well as pharmaceuticals.

HOLIDAYS
State holidays are held on the same date each year, but religious holidays fall on different dates each year in accordance with the lunar Hejira calendar (which is 11 days shorter than the Gregorian calendar used in the UK and elsewhere). Public holidays for 2012 and 2013:

New Year's Day 1 January
Manifesto of Independence 11 January
Aïd al-Mawlid (Prophet's Birthday) 4 February 2012, 24 January 2013, 13 January 2014
Labour Day 1 May
Feast of the Throne 30 July
Fête Oued Eddahab (Oued Eddahab Allegiance Day) 14 August
Aïd al-Fitr (End of Ramadan) 19 August 2012, 8 August 2013, 28 July 2014
Révolution du Roi et du Peuple (Anniversary of the King and the People's Revolution) 20 August
King Mohammed's Birthday 21 August
Aïd al-Adha (Feast of the Sacrifice) 26 October 2012, 15 October 2013, 4 October 2014
Marche Verte (Anniversary of the Green March) 6 November
Fatih Muharram (Muslim New Year) 15 November 2012, 4 November 2013
Fête de l'Indépendance (Independence Day) 18 November

INTERNET
Several hotels and riads offer wi-fi or computers with internet access. Otherwise, internet cafes ringing the Djemaa el-Fna are inexpensive (Dh8 to Dh12 per hour) and filled with locals flirting online. Most open by 10am and close around 11pm.

The main trouble-shooter in town for computer trouble is

KNK La Kasbah Numérik (Map p38-9, E2; ☎ 0524 434568; www.lakasbah-numerik .com; Ave du Prince Moulay Abdullah).

INTERNET CAFES
Cyber Bab Agnaou (Map p69, B6; Rue de Bab Agnaou; ☷ 9am-11pm) A dozen computers, with decent printers and scanners, downstairs in a shopping mall.
Cyber Café in Cyberpark (Map p38, F5; off Ave Mohammed V; ☷ 9.30am-7.30pm) Go figure: 15 terminals with fast connections in a royal rose garden.
Hassan Internet (Map p69, B6; ☎ 0524 441989; Immeuble Tazi, 12 Rue Riad el-Moukha; per hr Dh8; ☷ 7am-midnight) Near Tazi Hotel; 12 terminals.

USEFUL WEBSITES
Lonely Planet's own website, www.lonelyplanet.com, offers a speedy link to many websites on Morocco. See p132 for accommodation websites; other handy Marrakesh sites include the following:
Al-Bab (www.al-bab.com/maroc/trav/marra kesh.htm) Gateway to Marrakesh, covering current affairs, news and books about Morocco.
Amazigh Voice (www.amazigh-voice.com) Online Berber Pride forum, with articles on Berber culture, language and heritage in French and English.
Laila Lalami (www.lailalalami.com/blog) Insightful, topical blog by novelist Laila Lalami (who wrote *Hope and Other Dangerous Pursuits*) about Moroccan culture and politics.
Maghreb Arts (www.maghrebarts.ma) French-language coverage of Moroccan film, music, theatre, art exhibitions and other cultural events.

Maghreb Press (www.map.ma/eng) The latest official news from Morocco in English.
Speak Moroccan (www.speakmoroccan.com) A helpful website to pick up key phrases in Darija (Moroccan Arabic).

LANGUAGE
In Marrakesh, you'll hear six main languages spoken: Tashelhit (a local Berber dialect), Darija (Moroccan dialect Arabic), French, Fusha (classical Arabic), Spanish and English. For key phrases in Darija and Tashelhit see p82 and p101.

MONEY
For current exchange rates, see the inside front cover, but here are some key figures to factor into your travel budget: a tagine costs Dh30-plus; bottled water Dh5 to Dh8; an overnight stay in a riad Dh350-plus; a spa treatment at a public hammam Dh30 to Dh50.

TELEPHONE
Many European mobile phones work with Morocco's two GSM mobile-phone networks, but check with your carrier about roaming charges. Téléboutiques that sell phone cards and provide phone booths can be found all over town.

COUNTRY & CITY CODES
For international calls from Morocco, dial ☎ 00 then the country

code, the area code and the number. Morocco's country code is ☎ 212, followed by the area code minus the initial 0. Dial the ☎ 0524 area code even if you're calling from within Marrakesh. Mobile numbers often begin with ☎ 0661 or 0668.

USEFUL PHONE NUMBERS
International operator (☎ 120)
Local directory inquiries (☎ 160) If your French isn't so slick, ask your front-desk clerk for help.

TIPPING
Tipping is not only customary here, it's the bulk of many Marrakshi livelihoods. Tip waiters 10% to 15%, and leave a little something (Dh20 or so) for the riad staff who clean your room. In taxis, round up to the nearest dirham on the meter.

TOURIST INFORMATION
The **Office National du Tourisme Marocain** (Tourist Information Office; Map p39,

A7; ☎ 0524 436179; Place Abdel Moumen ben Ali, cnr Blvd Mohammed Zerktouni & Ave Mohammed V, Guéliz) is good for pamphlets and numbers of licensed guides, but not much else. For recommendations of where to go, ask at the place you're staying or talk to fellow travellers.

TRAVELLERS WITH DISABILITIES
Overall, Marrakesh gets a poor rating for accessibility, though this hasn't deterred a growing number of intrepid disabled travellers. Wheelchair access is only provided in a few hotels, and navigating rutted alleys and crowded souqs is difficult. The lack of traffic signals and right-of-way are dangers for those with sight, hearing or mobility impairments.

However, some notable attractions, along with restaurants and gardens, are accessible to disabled travellers, and Marrakshis do their utmost to accommodate all guests.

>INDEX

See also separate subindexes for See (p173), Shop (p173), Eat (p175), Drink (p175) and Play (p175).

000 map pages

000 map pages

000 map pages